TRACING BOARDS
OF THE
THREE DEGREES
IN
CRAFT
FREEMASONRY
EXPLAINED

JULIAN REES

Published 2015 by arima publishing

www.arimapublishing.com

ISBN 978 1 84549 661 6

© Julian Rees 2015

Printed and bound in the United Kingdom

Typeset in Garamond

arima publishing

ASK House, Northgate Avenue

Bury St Edmunds, Suffolk IP32 6BB

t: (+44) 01284 700321

www.arimapublishing.com

CONTENTS

ILLUSTRATIONS

70   18th century French third degree board from Delaulnay's *Thuileur. (Courtesy Library and Museum of Freemasonry, London)*

71   French third degree tracing board. *(Courtesy Jacques Thomas and Editions Dervy, Paris)*

72   Grande Loge de France temple interior. *(Courtesy Verlag Christian Brandstätter, Vienna. Photo: Laziz Hamani)*

73   Austrian lodge carpet 1780. *(Courtesy Wien Museum, Vienna, Austria. Photo: Enver Hirsch)*

74   A room in Schloß Rosenau, Austria. *(Courtesy Freimaurermuseum, Schloß Rosenau, Austria. Photo: Rüdiger Wolf)*

75   Austrian tracing boards first and second degrees, 21st century. *(Photo: Herbert Scbmid-Korlath)*

76   *left:* Austrian third degree tracing board, 21st century. *(Courtesy Freimaurer-museum, Schloß Rosenau, Austria. Photo: Rüdiger Wolf)*

      right: French tracing board *c.*1760. *(Courtesy Deutsches Freimaurermuseum, Bayreuth, Germany)*

77   German tracing board, mid-19th century. *(Courtesy Quatuor Coronati Lodge, Bayreuth, Germany)*

78   *upper:* German tracing board, mid-19th century. *(Courtesy Quatuor Coronati Lodge, Bayreuth, Germany)*

      lower: Lodge carpet for the Großloge Zu den Drei Weltkugeln, from 1960. *(Courtesy Quatuor Coronati Lodge, Bayreuth, Germany)*

79   Lodge carpet for the Großloge Zu den Drei Weltkugeln. *(Courtesy Quatuor Coronati Lodge, Bayreuth, Germany)*

80   Three Nordic Rite tracing boards, 18th century. *(Courtesy Quatuor Coronati Lodge, Bayreuth)*

81   Modern Nordic Rite first and second degree tracing board. *(Photo: Julian Rees)*

82   *left:* Frontispiece to *The Builders Jewel,* London 1741. *(Courtesy Library and Museum of Freemasonry, London)*

      right: Tracing board, New York, *c.*1800. *(Courtesy Chancellor Robert R. Livingston Masonic Library of Grand Lodge, New York. Photo: Catherine Walter)*

83   Lodge cloth, North Carolina, *c.*1770 *(Courtesy Royal White Hart Lodge and Museum of Early Southern Decorative Arts)*

84   Tracing board by Jonas Prentiss, 1818, West Cambridge, Massachusetts. *(Courtesy National Heritage Museum, Lexington, Massachusetts. Photo: David Bohl)*

85   Lodge cloth, Charlottesville, Virginia, *c.*1800. *(Courtesy Museum of Early Southern Decorative Arts, Salem, N. Carolina)*

86   'Master's Carpet Cornpleat', drawing by Thomas Kensett, Connecticut, 1812. *(Courtesy Connecticut Historical Society, Hertford, Connecticut)*

87   Tracing board, Western Star Lodge, No. 15, Bridgewater, New York. *(Courtesy Chancellor Robert R. Livingston Masonic Library of Grand Lodge, New York. Photo: Richard A. Vang)*

88   Tracing board, Cherry Valley Lodge, No. 334, Cherry Valley, New York. *(Courtesy Chancellor Robert R. Livingston Masonic Library of Grand Lodge, New York. Photo: Richard A. Vang)*

89-90   Three tracing boards of The International Order of Freemasonry Le Droit Humain. *(Courtesy The International Order of Freemasonry Le Droit Humain, British Federation. Photo: Julian Rees)*

91   *left:* Tracing board of the Quadrum Leonardi Lodge, Budapest, Hungary. *(Courtesy Ferenc Sebök)*

      right: Tracing board of the Iris Lodge, Liège, Belgium. *(Courtesy Ferenc Sebök)*

92-93   Three tracing boards designed by Lady Frieda Harris. *(Courtesy Andrew Drylie. Photo: Mark Dennis)*

ACKNOWLEDGEMENTS

My thanks go to all of the following: Gary Albert and Jennifer Bean Bower of the Museum of Early Southern Decorative Arts, Salem, North Carolina, USA; Michael Baigent, Editor of *Freemasonry Today*; Ric Carter of the Grand Lodge of North Carolina; Diane Clements and all the staff of the Library and Museum of Freemasonry, London; Robert Cooper, Librarian and Curator of the Grand Lodge of Scotland; Andrew Drylie, owner of the Frieda Harris tracing boards; Kevin Duffy of Letchworth's, London; Maureen Harper of the National Heritage Museum, Lexington, Massachusetts, USA; Hans Kummerer, Master of the Quatuor Coronati Lodge, Vienna, Austria; Irène Mainguy, Librarian of the Grand Orient de France, Paris; Pierre Mollier, Director of the Library and Museum of the Grand Orient de France, Paris; Professor William Moore of Boston University, USA; Brent Morris, Editor of *The Scottish Rite Journal of Freemasonry, Southern Jurisdiction*, USA; Thad Peterson, Assistant Director of the Deutsches Freimaurermuseum, Bayreuth, Germany; Andrew Peto and Bruce Young of the Pilgrim Lodge, No. 238, London; Brian Roberts of the International Order of Freemasonry Le Droit Humain; Tom Savini, Director of the Chancellor Robert R. Livingston Masonic Library of Grand Lodge, New York, USA; Herbert Schmid-Korlath of the Mozart Lodge, Vienna, Austria; Ferenc Sebök of Belgium; Dr. Jan Snoek of Heidelberg University, Germany; Dr. Susanne Winkler of the National Museum, Vienna, Austria; Dr. Rüdiger Wolf, Director of the Freimaurermuseum Schloß Rosenau, Austria. I am particularly grateful to Neville Barker Cryer, for pointing me in the direction of the staircase conundrum in the second degree, and for much information relating to King Solomon's Temple.

My overwhelming debt of gratitude goes to Terence Haunch, former Director of the Library and Museum of Freemasonry, London, for his most generous support, and for the wealth of material he has placed at my disposal. His book *Tracing Boards – Their Development and Their Designers* remains, after forty-six years, the seminal work *par excellence* on the subject. I feared to tread in the footsteps of this ultimate authority but he, generous as always, gave me encouragement, made the loan of priceless images of old tracing boards, and gave much more besides.

* * *

I dedicate this small work to the memory of Andrew Montgomery, known to many of us as Monty and to many more still as Brother Lightfoote of *Freemasonry Today*. He brought us the light of laughter and infused us with his true Masonic spirit.

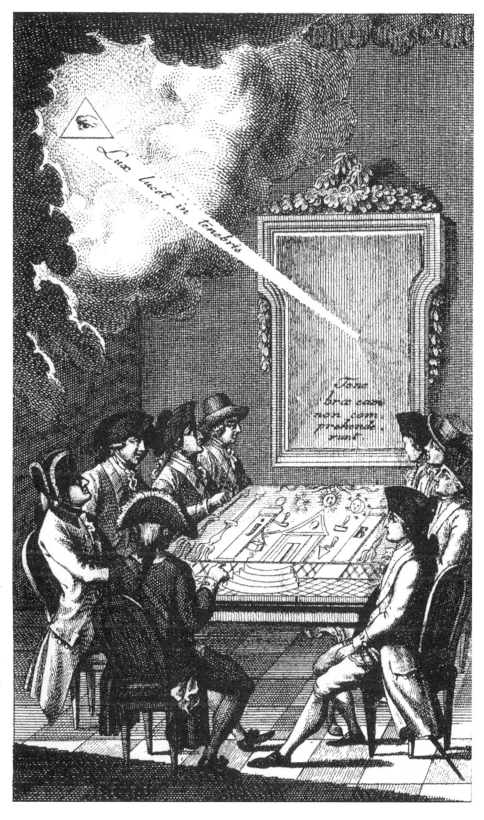

Frontispiece to Der Verklärte Freymaurer *(The Freemason Transfigured), Vienna, 1791. The two inscriptions, from the Gospel of St. John, Chapter 1, v.5 read 'Lux lucet in tenebris – tenebrae eam non comprehenderunt'. 'The light shineth in darkness; and the darkness comprehended it not.' The illustration is presumed to be a class of instruction, and the tracing board may be dated at between 1725 and 1744*

INTRODUCTION

Why tracing boards? Well, we can find rich justification for them from within the Masonic ritual itself. Historically too, we find accounts of our forebears tracing symbols on the floor of the lodge room, a practice that became codified and then embellished later to produce some examples of truly outstanding artistic achievement. And art, after all, is one of the glories which adorns the Masonic vocation; the second Emulation lecture speaks of painting and sculpture decorating 'the buildings fair science had raised, while the curious hand designed the furniture and tapestry, beautifying and adorning them …'

But why draw at all? Why trace anything? What does man achieve by recording in this way visual images of his surroundings, of his relationship to the world around him, visual images of the human condition? To understand this, we might go back to the earliest endeavours of man to depict images of his surroundings, images of his world and the objects in it, images of his own situation in his world. The earliest examples of art, those left to us by prehistoric man on the walls of caves, were a striving to fix transitory images in a way that he could then relate to. Once he had depicted, say, a bison in a static image on the wall of his cave, his companions may have been truly astonished to see, in the image, a representation of a material object normally found outside on the hunting fields, may indeed have been frightened by it, assuming the image to have the same qualities as the real object.

Later still, man learned to make manifest in such images some insights into non-material aspects of his existence, learned to portray qualities such as evil or goodness, emotions such as suffering or joy, love, fear, passion or kindness. He learned the value of tracing out for himself a picture of some project, to communicate his ideas in pictorial language to his companions, and to plan some design, a plan for a battle, a settlement, or the draft sketch for a building.

On a spiritual level also, man learned to render, in a form comprehensible to his fellow men, images in both sculpture and painting, images that would assist him in devotion to the deity. He created striking and poignant images of holy men and women, in all religions, images of holy persons, of saints, of God Himself, and to portray these images in a way that allowed him to focus his devotion and thereby assist him to gain access to celestial realms, and ultimately access to divinity in himself. These are evidenced by the statues and icons of Christianity, and in the mandalas of the Hindu and Buddhist religions. All of these may be employed for focusing attention of aspirants and adepts, as a spiritual teaching tool, for establishing a sacred space and as an aid to meditation. According to Professor David Fontana, the symbolic nature of statues and icons can help 'to access progressively deeper levels of the unconscious, ultimately assisting the meditator to experience a mystical sense of oneness with the ultimate unity from which the cosmos in all its manifold forms arises.'

When our Masonic forebears decided to adapt the plans of a concrete object such as a building, and to make of the building allegory a plan for moral, intellectual and spiritual development, the possibilities became boundless. A pillar became not only a support for a building, but also a support for moral, social and spiritual endeavours. The covering or ceiling became a canvas on which to depict the heavens. It became possible to depict a carved stone as representing a stage in man's own inner development. And the placing of one stone on another became an allegory for the construction of more than a physical temple: it became the allegory by which he was able to trace the building of his own character and through that, the building of a temple to humanity, a temple of humanity.

In this tracery, he was then able to portray, in a tangible way, other divine and spiritual values. Jacob's Ladder was then depicted as it was meant to be – connecting heaven and earth, with the blazing star at the summit indicating God, the ladder then being an emblem of the possibility of man's ascent to celestial realms.

The three Emulation lectures, one for each degree, are very instructive in the content and function of tracing boards, instruction that is useful to all Freemasons, even if they do not work Emulation ritual in their own Lodges. The fifth section of the first lecture contains the following exchange:

Q. Name the immovable jewels.

A. The tracing board, the rough and perfect ashlars.

Q. Their uses?

A. The tracing board is for the Master to lay lines and draw designs on; the rough ashlar for the Entered Apprentice to work, mark and indent on; and the perfect ashlar for the experienced craftsman to try, and adjust, his jewels on.

Q. Why are these called immovable jewels?

A. Because they lie open and immovable in the Lodge for the Brethren to moralise on.

What is more, there is ample evidence that, in the 18th century, much instruction was imparted to the candidate, not so much in the course of the degree ceremony, but afterwards, in the form of education, fitting the candidate for the subsequent degree. Such instruction seems to have fallen by the wayside. This is the only way we can explain why the candidate in the first degree is not instructed that the three grand principles on which the Order is founded are brotherly love, relief and truth – the Entered Apprentice only discovers this important information when he learns the questions leading to the second degree. Similarly, although the peculiar objects of the second degree are the hidden mysteries of nature and science, the Fellow Craft has to wait for this revelation until he studies the questions leading to the third degree. It is clear that we, in the 21st century, are missing something. Hence this book attempts to fill in some of the missing features – to complete the landscape.

The earliest practice of laying out the symbols for study in lodges seems to have been in the form of a drawing on the floor, using chalk or charcoal. In the 18th century, several exposures of Freemasonry were published, one of which was a publication entitled *Jachin and Boaz* which appeared in 1762, in which the following passage appears:

> *He* [the candidate] *is also learnt the Step or how to advance to the Master upon the Drawing on the Floor, which in some Lodges resembles the Grand Building, termed a Mosaic Palace and is described with the utmost exactness. They also draw other Figures, one of which is called the Lace Tuft, and the other the Throne beset with Stars ... The Ceremony being now ended the new-made Member is obliged to take a Mop out of a Pail of Water brought for that Purpose, and rub out the Drawing if it is done with Chalk or Charcoal ...*

In other words, they were exceedingly careful that the images they drew on the floor of the Lodge should not be seen by the profane world.

To sum up: Freemasonry is about rendering in symbol and allegory that which words alone cannot render. And a visual image gives us a way of using our own insight to de-code the message. The tracing boards are there to do just that – from their original function of laying out the plan of the building, they have developed into a means for us to lay out the message, and then to profit by it.

In a sense, this book is written back-to-front; we are going to examine the three Craft tracing boards first, laying out the allegories and symbols, then, as an adjunct, we will take a short look at the history of their development, looking at some older forms of the tracing boards in use long before the present-day Emulation boards were developed. After that we shall be looking at practices in other Masonic jurisdictions and other countries. But the first three chapters of this book deal with the Emulation tracing boards, since they are the most commonly used in England.

The tracing boards used in the Emulation Lodge of Improvement in London were designed and painted by John Harris in 1845 and measure approximately 183 cm (6 ft) by 91 cm (3 ft), measurements which have an allegorical significance in the third degree. Although these boards were painted by Harris expressly for the Emulation Lodge of Improvement, many copies of them were made, and these are the images reproduced in the ritual and lecture books of the Emulation working. However, it is interesting to note that a mere four years later, in 1849, Harris painted a different set in which, most importantly, a significant change was made to the second degree board, which is mentioned in this book in the chapter dealing with that degree.

When the building of the new Freemasons' Hall in London was completed in 1933, the boards commissioned for use in the individual lodge rooms were of a different design, reflecting the art deco influence of the period. The architects were commissioned to produce a new design on a simplified basis which would be more suitable for reproduction. In the first three chapters however, we shall be dealing with the Emulation or John Harris boards.

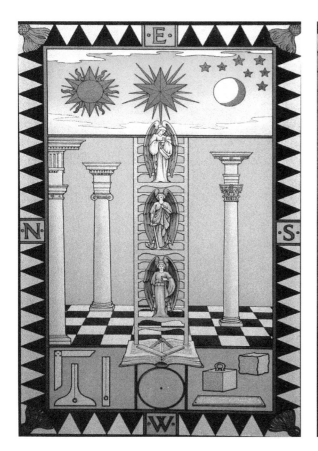

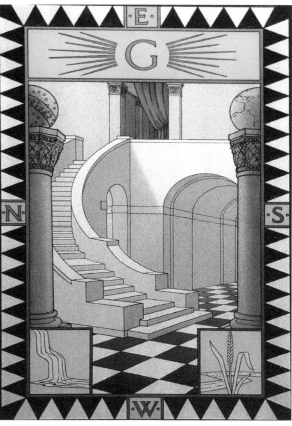

Tracing boards provided for the use of lodges in Freemasons' Hall, London

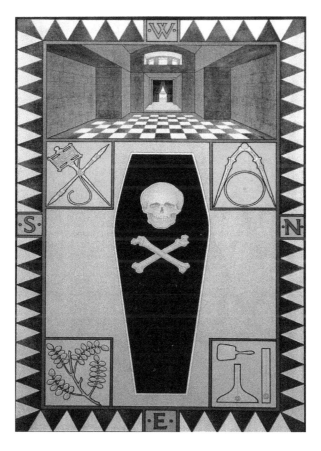

THE FIRST DEGREE

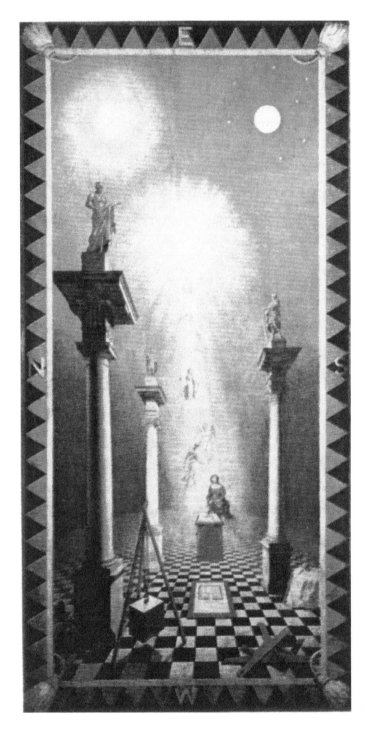

Emulation first degree
tracing board,
John Harris 1845

As soon as the newly-made Mason – the latest to enjoy the title of Entered Apprentice – has had a chance to look round the Temple and to take in some of the detail, his attention will be very quickly drawn to an object he will learn is called the tracing board. It will be displayed either on the floor in the middle of the Temple, as is the practice in the Emulation Lodge of Improvement in London, or standing upright against the Junior Warden's pedestal.

It will probably take a little longer than that for him to relate all of the symbols on the first degree board to the Temple itself, its ornaments, furniture and jewels. Later, he will find concurrences between the symbols on the board, and the contents of the Temple in which he has been made an Entered Apprentice. But unless the boards are very old or damaged, he will straight away be struck by the blaze of light, or more correctly, two brilliant light-sources depicted on the board: the blazing star and the sun. When John Harris designed this board it was no accident that the blazing star was painted brighter than the sun, an allegory that there is no power, no enlightenment more glorious than that of the Great Architect, not even the sun, the brightest material object in our solar system.

THE FEATURES OF THE BOARD

But we are getting ahead of ourselves. Let us first detail the features of this board, so that we can put them into some sort of order by which we can study them and work out their import and importance. First of all, we notice that the border is a zig-zag pattern, known as tesselation, an interlinking pattern of juxtaposed light and dark triangles, and on each side are marked the cardinal points of the compass, the positions of north, south, east and west. At each corner is a tassel. In those Lodges where the board is laid in the middle of the floor, it will be so oriented that the east side, the top as we look at it, will be towards the Master, and the west side towards the Senior Warden.

Now for the inner part, the detail. Apart from the sun in the top left-hand corner, and the blazing star at the top of the ladder, the moon is shown at the top right-hand corner surrounded by seven stars. The next most striking part of the board is the three pillars, the farthest one, the one nearest the Master, being of the Ionic Order, the nearest, western pillar, being of the Doric Order and the third one, on the right or south side, being of the Corinthian Order. A little further east from the Ionic pillar stands the Master's pedestal or altar. On the front of the altar are two parallel lines and between these is a point at the centre of a circle, a circle which touches on the two lines. Resting on the top of the altar is the Volume of the Sacred Law, the square and compasses, and resting on the Sacred Volume is the bottom of Jacob's Ladder. On the ladder are figures, in ascending order, of Faith, Hope and Charity, with angels interspersed between them.

Just in front of the altar, on the floor, is a depiction of a tracing board, a board within a board we might say. By the Corinthian pillar and therefore near to the Junior Warden in the south, is a rough-hewn stone, the rough ashlar mentioned in the ritual, and close to it or resting on it, a twenty-four-inch gauge, a gavel and a chisel. By the Doric pillar and therefore near to the Senior Warden in the west, is a smooth or 'dressed' stone, the perfect ashlar, supported on a derrick by means of a lewis or metal clamp inserted into the stone. To the left of that, on the floor and nearly out of sight, can be seen part of a winding gear or windlass to wind the cable lifting the stone supported on the derrick. And lastly, in the bottom right-hand corner of the board, a square, a level and a plumb rule lying together. All of these objects, from the altar in the east to the square, level and plumb rule in the west, stand on the squared or mosaic pavement of black and white squares. Indeed, if you look closely, you will see the squared pavement reaching back in the east to beyond the altar, implying that it has no end.

By far the most important emblem on this board is the blazing star. In the 18th century, in an age when it was important for Freemasonry to distance itself from religion, and from denominations within a religion, the blazing star became the symbol by which all Freemasons might recognise, and identify with, the Great Architect of the Universe.

THE FORM OF THE LODGE

It is in many ways a pity that the first-degree tracing board lecture is so seldom delivered in open Lodge. Like the Emulation first degree lecture, it contains much valuable information enabling us to de-code the first degree symbolism. One of the first statements in this lecture is that the form of the Lodge is

> *... a parallelopipedon, in length from east to west, in breadth from north to south, in depth from the surface of the earth to the centre, and even as high as the heavens.*

There are not many people who can tell you exactly what is a parallelopipedon. The most common dictionary definition is 'a prism whose bases are parallelograms'. A parallelogram is a two-dimensional, four-sided figure, with two sets of parallel sides. On that definition, any square or rectangle is a parallelogram. But a prism is a three-dimensional object, so we are here dealing with a three-dimensional figure having six faces. The term parallelopipedon counts as a surfeit of information, for the Lodge is simply a double cube, one which is as high as it is broad, and twice as long. So the floor area of the Lodge is a perfect rectangle, twice as long as it is broad, and these proportions are, not coincidentally, those of the tracing board itself.

We might note in passing that the double-cube form of the Lodge is a representation of what Hermes Trismegistus has to say: 'As above, so below, to achieve the wonders of the One', a reference to one-ness of God and man. Hence one cube represents the physical world, and the other represents the celestial realms. The interconnection of celestial and terrestrial is a theme we shall return to when speaking about Jacob's Ladder.

ORNAMENTS

The tesselated border thus contains the symbols of the board, in the same way that the tesselated border round the mosaic or chequered pavement in the Lodge contains the Lodge area itself. This border is the third of the ornaments of the Lodge, referred to in the tracing board lecture. The other two are the mosaic pavement and the blazing star.

The mosaic pavement

> *... may justly be deemed the beautiful flooring of a Freemason's Lodge, by reason of its being variegated and chequered. This points out the diversity of objects which decorate and adorn the creation, the animate as well as the inanimate parts thereof.*

This is expanded in the fifth section of the first degree lecture:

As the steps of man are trod in the various and uncertain incidents of life, and his days are variegated and chequered by a strange contrariety of events, his passage through this existence, though sometimes attended by prosperous circumstances, is often beset by a multitude of evils; hence is our Lodge furnished with mosaic work, to point out the uncertainty of all things here on earth ... Then while such emblems are before us, we are morally instructed not to boast of anything, but to give heed to our ways, to walk uprightly and with humility before God ...

The word mosaic has two meanings, each one in its way relevant to Freemasonry. The first dictionary definition is:

The process of producing pictures or patterns by cementing together small pieces of stone, glass etc. of various colours.

The second is:

Of, pertaining or relating to Moses, the lawgiver of the Hebrews ...

Hence mosaic law was the ancient law of the Hebrews, contained in the Pentateuch of the Old Testament.

The second of the three ornaments in the Lodge is the blazing star. There seems to be confusion about the nature of this emblem. The lecture tells us that

The blazing star, or glory in the centre, refers us to the sun, which enlightens the earth, and by its benign influence dispenses its blessings to mankind in general.

It is hard to square this with the tracing board itself however, since on the tracing board there is a quite separate emblem for the sun, and the emblem of the blazing star is situated at the top of Jacob's Ladder, the gateway to celestial realms, and therefore the presence of the Great Architect. Generally, the blazing star is taken as an image of the presence of the Great Architect of the Universe in Freemasonry throughout the world. According to Browne's *Master Key*, page 29, the blazing star reminds us of

... the omnipresence of the Almighty, overshadowing us with His Divine love and dispensing His blessings amongst us; and by being placed in the centre [of the Lodge] it ought to remind us that, wherever or however assembled, God the overseeing eye of providence is always in the midst of us, overseeing all our actions and observing the secret intents and movements of our hearts.

The indented or tesselated border is the third of the ornaments of the Lodge. According to the same section of the Emulation lecture, it

... refers us to the planets which, in their various revolutions, form a beautiful border or skirtwork round that grand luminary the sun, as the other does round that of a Freemason's Lodge.

This border, round the mosaic pavement or carpet in the temple, is that which binds the blazing star and the mosaic pavement together, emphasising the unity of the whole, the Divine world and the terrestrial, united. In the same way, you will notice that the tesselated border is the border of the tracing board itself, binding all the symbols together.

But on examination it proves to be more than this; at the corners are four tassels, denoting the four cardinal virtues, temperance, fortitude, prudence and justice. Temperance, in the sixth section of the first Emulation lecture, is defined as

> *... that due restraint of the passions and affections, which renders the body tame and governable ...*

Fortitude, we are told, is

> *... that noble and steady purport of the soul, which is equally distant from rashness and cowardice; it enables us to undergo any pain, labour, danger or difficulty ...*

Prudence teaches us

> *... to regulate our lives and actions according to the dictates of reason, and is that habit of mind whereby men wisely judge, and prudentially determine, all things relative to their temporal and eternal happiness.*

Justice is

> *... that station or boundary of right, by which we are taught to render to every man his just due, and that without distinction. This virtue is not only consistent with the divine and human law, but is the standard and cement of civil society.*

FURNITURE

The fifth section of the first Emulation lecture quoted above begins with the exchange:

Q. Of what is the interior of a Freemason's Lodge composed?

A. Ornaments, furniture and jewels.

It is a rather quaint 18th century expression, to speak of the 'furniture' of the Lodge. Broadly speaking, the meaning here is 'contents' and in that same lecture section we learn that the furniture consists of the Volume of the Sacred Law, the compasses and square. Note however that the order in which these are named is not the same as that in the first degree ceremony when describing the Great Lights. These three objects can be seen united on the altar, just below the figure of Faith at the bottom of Jacob's Ladder. In the degree ritual of course we know them as the three Great Lights, but here a slightly different slant is put on their symbolism:

> *The sacred writings are to rule and govern our faith; on them we obligate our candidates for Freemasonry. So are the compasses and square, when united, to regulate our lives and actions.*

In the first degree ceremony, immediately after the blindfold is removed, the Master will explain these three Great Lights to the candidate in a slightly different form. But here, in the literature of the tracing board, the explanation goes further. We learn of the association of these three articles of furniture, and their attachments.

Q. From whom is the first derived, and to whom do the other two more properly belong?

A. The sacred volume is derived from God to man in general, the compasses belong to the Grand Master in particular, and the square to the whole craft.

Q. Why the sacred volume from God to man in general?

A. Because the Almighty has been pleased to reveal more of His divine will in that holy book than he has by any other means.

Q. Why the compasses to the Grand Master in particular?

A. That being the chief instrument made use of in the formation of architectural plans and designs, is peculiarly appropriated to the Grand Master, as an emblem of his dignity; he being the chief, head and governor of the Craft.

Q. And why the square to the whole Craft?

A. The Craft being obligated within the square, are consequently bound to act thereon.

MOVABLE JEWELS

Now we come, in a sense, to the centre of the symbolism of the first degree. In the bottom right-hand corner of the board lie three architectural objects: a square, a level and a plumb rule. At first sight, many Freemasons take these to be the working tools in the second degree, and question why they should be on the first board at all. The answer is, that they are not working tools, but movable jewels. The explanation for them given here, in the fifth section of the Emulation lecture, is identical to that given for the working tools in the second degree ceremony:

The square is to try, and adjust, rectangular corners of buildings and assist in bringing rude matter into due form; the level to lay levels, and prove horizontals; the plumb-rule to try, and adjust, uprights while fixing them on their proper bases.

The question-master continues:

Q. It would appear from this that they are mere mechanical tools; why do you call them jewels?

A. On account of their moral tendency, which renders them jewels of inestimable value.

The passage which then follows, in which the movable jewels are moralised, is one of the most beautiful passages in English Masonic literature, too long to repeat here. At the end, we learn that they are called movable jewels because they are worn by the Master and his Wardens, and are transferred to their successors on nights of installation. The Master, we are told, is distinguished by the square.

> *As it is by the assistance of the square that rude matter is brought into due form, so it is by the square conduct of the Master that animosities are made to subside, should any unfortunately arise among the Brethren, that the business of Masonry may be conducted with harmony and decorum.*

The square then, far from being an active building implement such as a gavel, chisel or trowel, is an implement of quality control, by which the construction work, in the speculative sense as well as the operative, may be checked to see that it is progressing correctly.

The level, decorating the Senior Warden, is an emblem of equality, pointing out the equal measures he is bound to pursue in conjunction with the Master in the well-ruling and governing of the Lodge. The plumb rule, the emblem of the Junior Warden, points out integrity and uprightness. So all three are implements verifying the quality of the work, operative or speculative.

IMMOVABLE JEWELS

Halfway between the front of the scene on the board and the altar, roughly in a line across from mid-south to north west, are situated the immovable jewels, which are the tracing board in the middle of the picture, the rough ashlar or rough-hewn stone on the right by the Corinthian pillar, and the perfect ashlar or dressed stone by the Doric pillar on the left. These are called immovable jewels because they 'lie open and immovable in the Lodge for the Brethen to moralise on'. These are central to the moral improvement to which each Freemason aspires, and the fifth section of the first Emulation lecture illustrates them by comparing them with the furniture of the Lodge described above.

> *As the tracing board is for the Master to lay lines and draw designs on, the better to enable the Brethren to carry on the intended structure with regularity and propriety, so the Volume of the Sacred Law may justly be deemed the spiritual tracing board of the Great Architect of the Universe, in which are laid down such divine laws and moral plans, that were we conversant therein and adherent thereto, would bring us to an ethereal mansion not made with hands, eternal in the heavens. The rough ashlar is a stone, rough and unhewn as taken from the quarry, until, by the industry and ingenuity of the workman, it is modelled, wrought into due form, and rendered fit for the intended structure. This represents man in his infant or primitive state, rough and unpolished as that stone, until, by the kind care and attention of his parents or guardians, in giving him a liberal and virtuous education, his mind becomes cultivated, and he is thereby rendered a fit member of civilised society. The perfect ashlar is a stone of a true die or square, fit only to be tried by the square and compasses. This represents man in the decline of years, after a regular well-spent life in acts of piety and virtue, which can no otherwise be tried and approved than by the square of God's word, and the compass of his own self-convincing conscience.*

The rough ashlar is shown with the twenty-four-inch gauge leaning against it and, although very small, one can just discern, resting on the stone, the common gavel and the chisel, and this is of course where moral improvement in a Masonic sense begins, since these are the three working tools of an Entered Apprentice or first degree Mason. The twenty-four-inch gauge is to measure the work, the common gavel to knock off the irregularities as a first stage to rendering the stone smooth, and the chisel to achieve the fine work necessary in the 'dressing' of the stone to make of it a perfect ashlar. In a speculative sense, the ritual tells us, the twenty-four-inch gauge

> *... represents the twenty-four hours of the day, part to be spent in prayer to Almighty God, part in labour and refreshment, and part in serving a friend or Brother in time of need ... the common gavel represents the force of conscience, which should keep down all vain and unbecoming thoughts which might obtrude during any of the aforementioned periods, so that our words and actions may ascend unpolluted to the throne of grace. The chisel points out to us the advantages of education, by which means alone we are rendered fit members of regularly- organised society.*

PERFECT ASHLAR

The perfect ashlar, which results from such work both operatively and speculatively, is shown on the board suspended from a derrick, and indeed on many Senior Wardens' pedestals such a derrick is present, but it is not mandatory in Lodges, and often the perfect ashlar is present on the pedestal, plain, unadorned and not supported in this way.

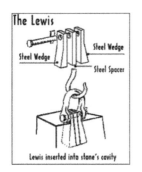

Before we leave the perfect ashlar, there is one more important aspect of it: the lewis. The dictionary defines a lewis as 'an iron contrivance for lifting heavy blocks of stone, consisting of three pieces dove-tailed together. Also called lewisson'. As the diagram shows, it is a remarkably sleek and efficient way of lifting stones. A dovetail cavity is first carved into the stone at the top. The two iron wedges are dropped into this cavity and spread apart, then the iron spacer is inserted in between them. All three are then secured with a bolt to the shackle, which is attached to a hawser or rope for lifting purposes. The seventh section of the lecture has the following exchange:

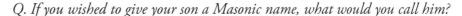

> *Q. If you wished to give your son a Masonic name, what would you call him?*
>
> *A. Lewis.*
>
> *Q. What does Lewis denote?*
>
> *A. Strength.*
>
> *Q. How is it depicted in our Lodges?*
>
> *A. By certain pieces of metal dovetailed into a stone, forming a cramp; and when in combination with some of the mechanical powers, such as a system of pulleys, it enables the operative Mason to raise great weights to certain heights with little encumbrance, and to fix them on their proper bases.*
>
> *Q. Lewis being the son of a Mason, what is his duty to his aged parents?*
>
> *A. To bear the heat and burden of the day which they, by reason of their age, ought to be exempt from; to assist them in time of need, and thereby render the close of their days happy and comfortable.*

Q. His privilege for so doing?

A. That of being made a Mason before any other person, however dignified.

PILLARS

We spoke earlier about the two bright light sources on the board – the sun and the blazing star. Apart from those, by far the most prominent objects on the board are the three pillars: the Ionic pillar in the east identifying the position of the Master, the Doric in the west that of the Senior Warden, and the Corinthian in the south that of the Junior Warden. There are three figures surmounting the three pillars: that in the east the figure of Solomon King of Israel, in the west that of Hiram King of Tyre, and in the south that of Hiram Abiff. There are two approaches to the explanation of these pillars. In the first degree ceremony, they are referred to by the Master as the three Lesser Lights, which

> *… are situated east, south and west, and are meant to represent the sun* [in the south, at midday], *the moon* [in the west, at sunset], *and Master of the Lodge* [in the east]; *the sun to rule the day, the moon to govern the night, and the Master to rule and direct his Lodge.*

The second approach is that contained in the tracing board lecture, or the fourth section of the first Emulation lecture, where they are named by virtues or qualities, apart from their references to the sun, moon and Master mentioned above.

Q. What supports a Freemason's Lodge?

A. Three great pillars.

Q. What are they called?

A. Wisdom, strength and beauty.

Q. Why wisdom, strength and beauty?

A. Wisdom to contrive, strength to support and beauty to adorn.

We are then told the function of these virtues or qualities:

> *Wisdom to conduct us in all our undertakings, strength to support us under all our difficulties, and beauty to adorn the inward man. The universe is the temple of the Deity whom we serve; wisdom, strength and beauty are about His throne as pillars of His works, for His wisdom is infinite, His strength omnipotent, and beauty shines through the whole of the creation in symmetry and order. The heavens He has stretched forth as a canopy; the earth He has planted as a footstool; He crowns His temple with stars as with a diadem, and with His hand he extends the power and glory.*

And this is where the principal objects on the board begin to be drawn together to make a coherent whole:

> *The sun and moon are messengers of His will, and all his law is concord. The three great pillars supporting a Freemason's Lodge are emblematic of those divine attributes, and further represent Solomon King of Israel, Hiram King of Tyre and Hiram Abiff.*

The first of these, King Solomon, is represented for his wisdom in building, completing and dedicating the temple at Jerusalem to God's service; Hiram King of Tyre for his strength in supporting him with men and materials; Hiram Abiff for his curious and masterly workmanship in beautifying and adorning the temple.

THE ALTAR

The altar is positioned on the mosaic pavement in the centre background, and is of course that object normally associated in a lodge room with the Master's pedestal. In most Lodges in the world, especially outside those jurisdictions directly descended from the United Grand Lodge of England, there is present in the Lodge a quite separate altar, standing near the centre, that is to say between the Secretary's table and the Junior Warden's pedestal. But from the perspective of Emulation, the Master's pedestal and the altar are one and the same. This altar has traced on its front a circle bounded by two vertical parallel lines, and with a point at the centre of the circle.

The first-degree tracing board lecture has this to say:

> *In all regular, well-formed, constituted Lodges, there is a point within a circle round which the Brethren cannot err; this circle is bounded between north and south by two grand parallel lines, one representing Moses, and the other King Solomon …*

Now we may recall what we had to say about the mosaic pavement, namely that in one sense it refers us to Moses, the law-giver. Moses received from God the ten commandments, the divine law. King Solomon it was who then dispensed the divine law to humankind, so these two parallel lines represent the receiving and the giving of God's law to man. In the USA, the ritual pre-dates the union of the two Grand Lodges in England, and there these two parallel lines represent the two Saints John, one of them Saint John the Baptist, the patron saint of Freemasonry, whose feast falls on midsummer day, the 21st of June, and the other Saint John the Evangelist, whose feast falls on midwinter day, the 21st of December.

JACOB'S LADDER

We noted earlier that the altar supports the Bible, and as we can see on the board, the Bible supports Jacob's Ladder. This aspect of the board relates to the fourth section of the Emulation first lecture:

> *Q. Name the covering of a Freemason's Lodge.*

> *A. A celestial canopy of divers colours, even the heavens.*

> *Q. As Masons, how do we hope to arrive there?*

> *A. By the assistance of a ladder, in scripture called Jacob's Ladder.*

There then follows the legend of Jacob's Ladder, of how Jacob, fleeing the wrath of his brother, went into the desert, and when he lay down to sleep he had a dream. In this dream he saw a ladder, the top of which reached to the heavens, and the angels of the Lord ascending, taking petitions from humankind to the Almighty, and other angels descending, dispensing God's blessing to humankind. This is why the blazing star, the presence of God at the gateway to celestial realms, is shown at the top of the ladder. In Masonic lore three figures have been added to the ladder which are, in ascending order, those of Faith, Hope and Charity.

Jacob's Ladder rests on the Volume of the Sacred Law, which is itself in contact with the top of the circle on the front of the altar. The first-degree tracing board lecture tells us that

> *... in going round this circle, we must necessarily touch on both those parallel lines, likewiseon the Sacred Volume, and while a Mason keeps himself thus circumscribed, he cannot err.*

and the ladder rests on the Volume of the Sacred Law because

> *... by the doctrines contained in that Holy Book, we are taught to believe in the dispensations of divine providence, which belief strengthens our faith ...*

Faith is defined in the lecture as 'the foundation of justice, the bond of amity and the chief support of civil society'. Hope is 'an anchor of the soul both sure and steadfast, and enters into that within the veil'. Charity is 'the brightest ornament which can adorn our Masonic profession. It is the best test and surest proof of the sincerity of our religion'. The Mason who is possessed of this virtue

> *... may justly be deemed to have attained the summit of his profession ... an ethereal mansion, veiled from mortal eyes by the starry firmament, emblematically depicted in our Lodges by seven stars, which have an allusion to as many regularly-made Masons, without which no Lodge is perfect ...*

and these seven stars are now shown surrounding the image of the moon in the top right corner of the board.

Thus the first degree board leads us, from the mosaic pavement on the ground, past the movable and immovable jewels, the pillars, the altar and the Volume of the Sacred Law, to the ladder which, once we have ascended it, leads us to the stars and the heavenly realms, into the presence of the Great Architect of the Universe.

THE SECOND DEGREE

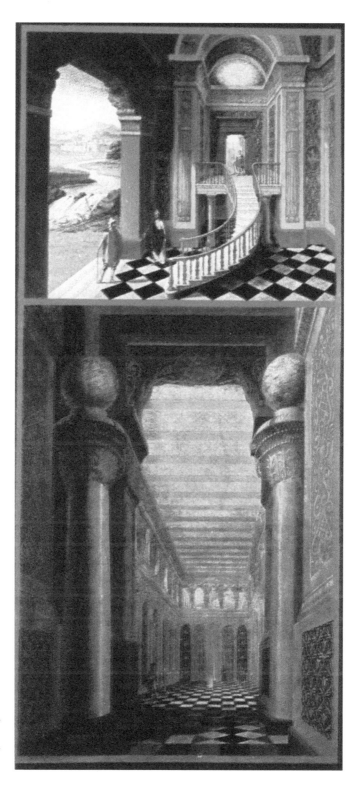

*Emulation second degree
tracing board,
John Harris 1845*

There is no better introduction to the second degree in Freemasonry than the words of the Master in the exhortation, which are here, paradoxically, not spoken until the third degree:

> *Proceeding onwards* [from the first degree], *still guiding your progress by the principles of <u>moral</u> truth, you were led in the second degree to contemplate the <u>intellectual</u> faculty, and to trace it from its development, through the paths of heavenly science, even to the throne of God Himself. The secrets of nature and the principles of intellectual truth were then unveiled to your view.*

This passage, with its emphasis upon the intellectual faculty, should remind us that organised Freemasonry found its origins in one of the most important intellectual and philosophical movements in Europe: the Age of Enlightenment.

THE AGE OF ENLIGHTENMENT

This is a term used to describe the outstanding development in Western philosophy and cultural life which arose, roughly speaking, in the years between the middle of the 17th century and lasted more or less until the early years of the 19th. This, in broad terms, was a period in which Reason came to be promoted as the primary source and basis of authority, in opposition to the almost unfettered domination wielded until then by the aristocracy, the establishment, and the church, authorities which were regarded by thinking men as reactionary and oppressive. It was a movement which had its origins in Germany, France and Britain but spread quickly. The signatories to the American *Declaration of Independence* and the French *Declaration des Droits de l'Homme et du Citoyen* (Declaration of the Rights of Man and of the Citizen), a fundamental document of the French Revolution, were motivated by Enlightenment principles.

The term Enlightenment represents more a set of attitudes than a set of ideas. At its core was a critical questioning of traditional institutions, customs and morals. The early period of the Enlightenment, the late 17th century, is also known as the Age of Reason. But, crucially for us, the establishment of the premier Grand Lodge of England in 1717 came at the very time of the rise of the Enlightenment. It is perhaps hard for us today to realise that the Freemasons of that time were radicals, and for many of them the Lodge was a haven where free thought and expression were possible in a way that would not have been possible in public.

The philosopher Spinoza (1632-1677) put forward a pantheistic view of the universe where God and nature were one, an idea that became central to the Enlightenment from Isaac Newton through to Thomas Jefferson. The Enlightenment is held to be the source of the idea that freedom, democracy and reason are central to the primary values of society. Because the Enlightenment contained so many contradictory themes, the philosopher Immanuel Kant described it simply as 'freedom to use one's own intelligence'. In an age where the spiritual and temporal powers sought to impose their will on the people, Kant's dictum was 'Aude sapere!' – 'Dare to know!'

All this is a rather long way of highlighting the importance of the second degree in Freemasonry. One of the themes central to this degree is 'the hidden mysteries of nature and science', so here we can see a direct connection with what was going on in the Age of Enlightenment, where men were, in effect, learning to think for themselves, and sometimes, in so doing, pitting themselves against the establishment and the church.

THE SECOND DEGREE BOARD

A first glimpse of the second degree tracing board is a little confusing. It is divided into two seemingly unrelated pictures – that at the top is unmistakably a depiction of the winding staircase leading to the middle chamber of King Solomon's Temple, while the lower two-thirds of the picture shows in splendid perspective the pillars at the east end of the temple, together with the vista looking westwards. Let us blend these two together by following the symbolism through in the order laid down in the second tracing board lecture.

TWO PILLARS

The lecture first points out the two great pillars which were placed at the porchway or entrance to the temple. That on the left was called Boaz and that on the right Jachin. We need to note that, in line with the teaching of the Emulation Lodge of Improvement in London, the left hand is intended to refer to the pillar on the left when looking out of the temple from inside. The pillar called Boaz is therefore on the right when looking at the board. The lecture describes in some detail the adornments of the pillars, and the fact that Solomon ordered them to be set up to remind the children of Israel of their deliverance from the state of slavery to which they had been subject in Egypt. The event is recorded in the seventh section of the first Emulation lecture, in which Moses was commanded by God to lead the Israelites towards the land of Canaan, which God had promised them for an inheritance.

The exodus from Egypt of the Israelites is a moral of triumph over adversity. When they arrived at the Red Sea they found that they could go no further, being hemmed in on left and right by mountains. Retreat was also impossible, since they were being pursued by the Egyptians. What follows is one of the Old Testament miracles. In the book of Exodus, Chapter 14, we read:

> *And Moses stretched out his hand over the sea; and the Lord caused the sea to go back by a strong east wind all that night, and made the sea dry land, and the waters were divided.*

The symbolism is dealt with in the seventh section of the first Emulation lecture:

Q. How blows the wind in Freemasonry?

A. Favourably, due east or west.

Q. For what purpose?

A. To cool and refresh men at labour.

Q. It has a further allusion.

A. To that miraculous wind, which proved so essential in working the happy deliverance of the children of Israel from their Egyptian bondage.

Later in the same chapter of the book of Exodus, we read that:

> *... the children of Israel went into the midst of the sea upon the dry ground: and the waters were a wall unto them on their right hand, and on their left. And the Egyptians pursued, and went in after them to the midst of the sea ... And it came to pass that in the morning watch the Lord looked unto the host of the Egyptians through the pillar of fire and of the cloud ... and took off their chariot wheels, that they drave them heavily ... and the Lord said unto Moses, Stretch out thine hand over the sea, that the waters may come again upon the Egyptians ... and Moses stretched forth his hand over the sea, and the sea returned to his strength ... and the Lord overthrew the Egyptians in the midst of the sea.*

The seventh section of the first Emulation lecture takes up this theme. The moral of the story is that, in the greatest adversity, if we put our trust in God, although a solution to that adversity may not be apparent, our trust is essential to our wellbeing, and is not a misplaced trust.

THE WINDING STAIRCASE

By far the most important part of the symbolism of this board is that which relates the ascent to the middle chamber. The lecture tells us that

> *... the Entered Apprentices received a weekly allowance of corn, wine and oil – the Fellow Crafts were paid their wages in specie, which they went to receive in the middle chamber of the Temple. They got there by the porchway or entrance on the south side.*

The Fellow Crafts engaged in the construction of the Temple therefore received payment of their wages in money, recompense for operative stonemasonry. Since we are here concerned with speculative Freemasonry, that recompense will be of a spiritual worth. It is reasonable to suppose that, in order to receive the benefit of spiritual grace, the Fellow Craft going to the middle chamber of the temple in a speculative sense will do so also to earn these spiritual benefits, and his journey to that place, a sacred place of worship, will entail not only payment to him of his spiritual wages, but also restitution by him of his debts in order to receive those wages. We need on many occasions to atone for past transgressions, repay old debts owed by us, and to put right any wrongs we may have done to others. Once we view the ascent to the middle chamber in this light, its value becomes more clear than ever.

A DIFFERENCE OF INTERPRETATION

We mentioned at the beginning the confusion in the depiction of the second board. In fact, there is ample evidence to show that John Harris made a mistake in his boards painted in 1845, in showing that access to the foot of the winding staircase was from the outside. The second degree board he painted in 1849 shows a view just inside the east entrance to the Holy Place, indicating the porchway on the south side giving out on to the north side of the outer courtyard. The foot of the staircase is shown, with the Junior Warden standing near it. The staircase winds up and to the left, but turns not through 90o as is indicated on the earlier board, but through 180o, in order

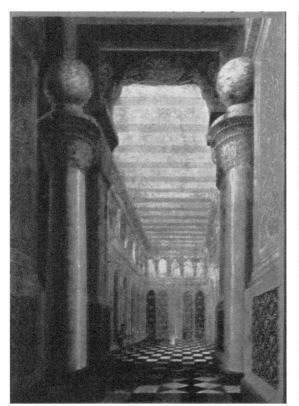
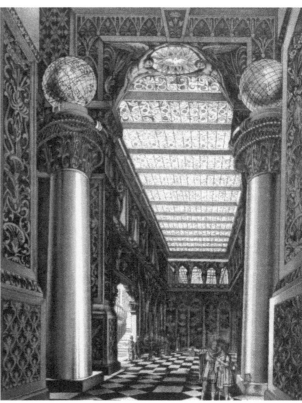

Above left and right:
John Harris second
degree board 1845 ...

... and his second degree
board 1849

then to give access, eastwards, to the middle chamber on the upper level. And indeed it is the custom in some Lodges for the aspirant to step off from the north, shortly to the west, and then to curve round in 180° to face the Master's pedestal in the east.

PROVING

Before ascending the winding staircase, it is necessary to prove entitlement to do so, namely the transition from the first to the second degree, and the Brother aspiring to be passed to the second degree proves himself in this way, with the password, to the Junior Warden, the figure standing at the foot of the stairway.

A shibboleth is a practice which is indicative of social or regional origin. However, it usually refers to language usage. More specifically, it is any word whose pronunciation identifies its speaker as being a member, or not, of a particular group. The term originates from the Hebrew word which literally means the part of a plant containing grains, such as an ear of corn or a stalk of grain or, in different contexts, 'stream' or 'torrent'. It derives from an account in the Hebrew Bible, in which pronunciation of this word was used to distinguish the Ephraimites, whose dialect lacked a 'sh' sound, from the Gileadites, whose dialect did include such a sound. In the Old Testament Book of Judges, after the inhabitants of Gilead inflicted a military defeat on the tribe of Ephraim (around 1370- 1070 BC), the surviving Ephraimites tried to cross the Jordan River back into their home territory, and the Gileadites secured the river's fords to stop them. In order to identify and kill these disguised refugees, the Gileadites put each refugee to a simple test.

As far as our tracing board is concerned, we can indeed see, just outside the porchway, an ear of corn at the side of a waterfall, thus depicting both senses of the Hebrew word.

ASCENDING

There are, in many places in the world, mazes or labyrinths laid out on the floors of churches, cathedrals, temples and other sacred places. One of the most striking of these is at Chartres Cathedral in France. In order to explore these labyrinths, and in order to find the centre, the seeker has to perambulate in a more or less circular fashion, turning as the alleyways in the maze direct. Each time he turns, the seeker sees the objects around him from a different angle. So it is with ascending this winding staircase. The aspirant commences, on the first four or five steps, facing the wall opposite and therefore viewing the rich wall decoration. As he gradually turns to the left his perspective changes: first he sees the cornice at the top of the wall, then the square pillar, then the bannister at the top of the staircase, and finally the passage leading to the door of the middle chamber, and the doorway itself.

DIFFERENT PERSPECTIVE

So it is also with the figurative ascent of the candidate completing his five steps in front of the Master's pedestal. His perspective changes until, at the altar itself, he comes face to face with the Master, and views the Volume of the Sacred Law lying before him, with the altered position of the square and compasses, another example of altered perspective. He is now made a Fellow Craft and allegorically gains entrance to the middle chamber, there to pay his debts and receive his wages. We have in fact many examples in Masonic lore of how necessary it is to change our perspective. For instance, in all three degrees, there is no coherent explanation for the disarranging of the candidate's clothing. The candidate enters the lodge room, blindfolded, with only one sleeve, only one leg covered, only one foot shod, his shirt open and all his money and valuables taken from him. If we view that as the frailty of the human condition until, having made moral and spiritual progress he becomes more stable in himself, then it has an added value for us.

Another cogent allegory is that in the second degree, namely the allegory of the hidden mysteries of nature and science. You may ask, since when were 'nature' and 'science' mysteries? And why should they be hidden? If we shift our perspective, and think of nature as our *own* nature, and think of science as the *knowing* of that nature, and consider then that self-knowledge follows from our uncovering, *discovering* our own nature which may be hidden under layers of impediments which modern life lays on it, then we gain enlightenment enabling a richer view.

At the top of the winding staircase, the aspirant arrives at the door of the middle chamber where, since he is now in possession of those marks entitling him to the privileges of a Fellow Craft, he is able to satisfy the Senior Warden, the figure standing by the open door. He may now enter, and be spiritually rewarded for the moral and spiritual work he has accomplished in his own pursuit of self-knowledge. Note that, above the doorway leading to the middle chamber, the blazing star or glory, the emblem of the presence of God, is once again prominent.

ALLEGORY OF THE STAIRWAY

The second degree board is as remarkable for what has been left out, as for what has been included. The staircase is the only allegory on the board of the five noble orders of architecture and the seven liberal arts and sciences. As the lecture points out to us, the staircase is composed of three, five, seven or more steps, and these are of crucial significance. Three rule a Lodge, five hold a Lodge and seven or more make it perfect. The three who rule a Lodge are the Master and the two Wardens; the five who hold a Lodge are those three plus two Fellow Crafts; the seven who make it perfect are those five plus two Entered Apprentices. The lecture continues:

> *Three rule a Lodge because there were but three Grand Masters who bore sway at the building of the first Temple at Jerusalem, namely Solomon King of Israel, Hiram King of Tyre and Hiram Abiff.*

Here we have once again the three principal personalities who were adorned with a different allegory in the first degree: the three great pillars supporting a Freemason's Lodge, otherwise called wisdom, strength and beauty. But the five noble orders of architecture are not expanded on; they are only indicated by the number of steps, namely five.

FIVE ORDERS OF ARCHITECTURE

> *Five hold a Lodge in allusion to the five noble orders of architecture, namely the Tuscan, Doric, Ionic, Corinthian and Composite.*

We spoke earlier at some length about the Age of Enlightenment. One of the characteristics of Enlightenment thought was an adherence to Graeco-Roman architecture, and an attempt to recapture some of the glory of ancient cultures. So it was that, in the era in the 18th century when Freemasonry was on the rise, a major part of architectural projects throughout the western world, and in the new world, concentrated on imitating what had been done one and a half millennia before in ancient Greece and Rome.

Illustration of the principal features of the Doric Order

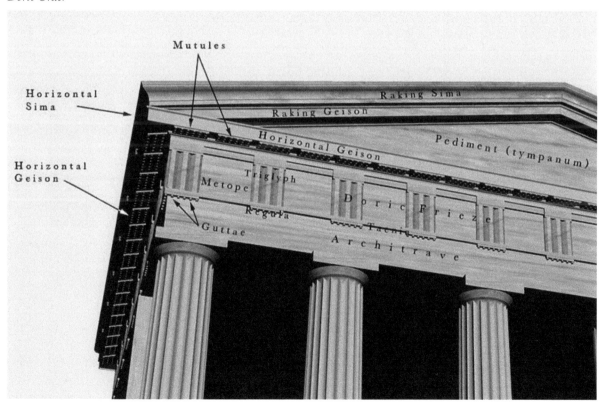

For a full explanation of the development of these orders of architecture, we must turn to the fourth section of the second Emulation lecture. This section asserts, with some justification, that the development of these orders has gone hand in hand with the rise of civilisation itself. It asserts that, when stone buildings began to supplant the wooden structures of the primitive world, the designs of the stone columns imitated the

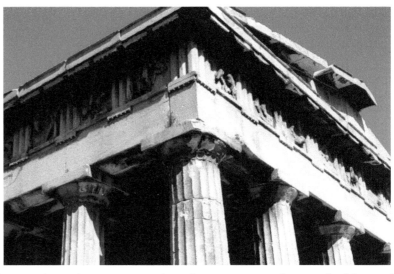

An example of decorated metopes

various parts of the wooden buildings. The orders are, in order of increasing elaboration, the Tuscan, Doric, Ionic, Corinthian and Composite. The Doric Order, that which distinguishes the Senior Warden in the Lodge, is the oldest of the five.

The entablature of an order of architecture is made up of three parts: the architrave, or beam, the frieze above it, and the cornice above that, underneath the roof. The frieze of the Doric Order is distinguished by triglyphs, which are vertically channelled tablets, separated by metopes, which are rectangular architectural elements filling the space between the triglyphs. The metopes are often decorated. The triglyphs represent the ends of the joists in the earlier wooden structures, and the mutules represent the ends of the rafters. The lecture tells us that

> *... the composition of this order is both grand and noble. Being formed after the model of a muscular, full-grown man, delicate ornaments are repugnant to its characteristic solidity. It therefore succeeds best in the regularity of its proportions and is principally used ... where strength and a noble simplicity are required.*

We may remember, from the first degree tracing board, that this, the second of the three great pillars supporting a Freemason's Lodge, represents strength. The next order, the Ionic, has its capital decorated by volutes, which are the spiral, scroll-like ornaments under the architrave at the top of the column. The temple of Diana at Ephesus in modern-day Turkey was composed of this order, the volutes representing a woman's flowing hair. This order, distinguishing the Master of the Lodge, thus emphasises the duality, masculine and feminine, in human nature. The order is

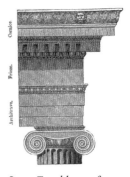

Ionic Entablature from the Temple of Minerva Polias at Priene

> *... formed after the model of a beautiful young woman, of an elegant shape, dressed in her hair, as a contrast to that of the Doric, which represents a strong, robust man.*

The third of the orders which feature in the interior of the Lodge is the Corinthian. It is said that this order was conceived by Calimachus, who lived c.305-240 bc, a native of the Greek colony of Cyrene, Libya. He was a noted poet, critic and scholar at the Library of Alexandria. The Corinthian Order is distinguished by two rows of leaves and eight volutes. Calimachus, it is said,

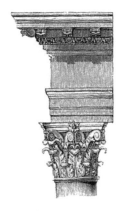

*Corinthian Capital
with Entablature from
the Pantheon at Rome*

accidentally passed by the tomb of a young lady, when he

> *… perceived a basket of toys which had been left there by her nurse, covered with a tile, and placed over an acanthus root; as the leaves grew up, they encompassed the basket, till arriving at the tile, they met with an obstruction and bent downwards. Calimachus, struck with the object, set about imitating the figure; the vase of the capital he made to represent the basket, the abacus the tile, and the volutes the bending leaves.*

This order distinguishes the Junior Warden and represents also the third of the three great pillars supporting a Freemason's Lodge, namely beauty.

In the degree ceremonies neither the Tuscan Order nor the Composite Order are mentioned. They are however dealt with in the fourth section of the second Emulation lecture:

> *The Tuscan Order is the simplest and most solid, and is placed first in the list of the five orders of architecture on account of its plainness. Its column is seven diameters high, the base, capital and entablature have but few mouldings and no other ornaments, whence it has been compared to a sturdy labourer dressed in homely apparel … there is a peculiar beauty in its simplicity which adds to its value and renders it fit to be used in structures where the rich and more delicate orders might be deemed superfluous.*

The Composite Order is so named

> *… from being composed of parts of the other orders. Its capital is adorned with the two rows of leaves of the Corinthian, the volutes of the Ionic, and has the quarter round of the Tuscan and Doric Orders. This order is chiefly used in structures where strength, elegance and beauty are displayed.*

LIBERAL ARTS AND SCIENCES

As with the five noble orders of architecture, the seven liberal arts and sciences are only indicated by the number of steps, in this case seven or more.

> *Seven or more make a perfect Lodge because King Solomon was seven years and upwards in building, completing and dedicating the temple at Jerusalem to God's service. They have likewise a further allusion to the seven liberal arts and sciences, namely grammar, rhetoric, logic, arithmetic, geometry, music and astronomy.*

If our Enlightenment forebears were enthusiastic about classical art and architecture, and the whole range of cultural achievements which accompanied them, they were no less engaged in other cerebral pursuits. In 1579, even before the period we regard as the Enlightenment, the Gresham College was founded in London for the teaching of divinity, law, astronomy, music, geometry, rhetoric and physics, a list with which the above liberal arts and sciences have a certain resonance. Gresham College was the precursor of the Royal Society, of which Christopher Wren was a member, as was Isaac Newton, and Jean Théophile Desaguliers, the third Grand Master of the Premier Grand Lodge of England, holding that post in 1719 and 1720.

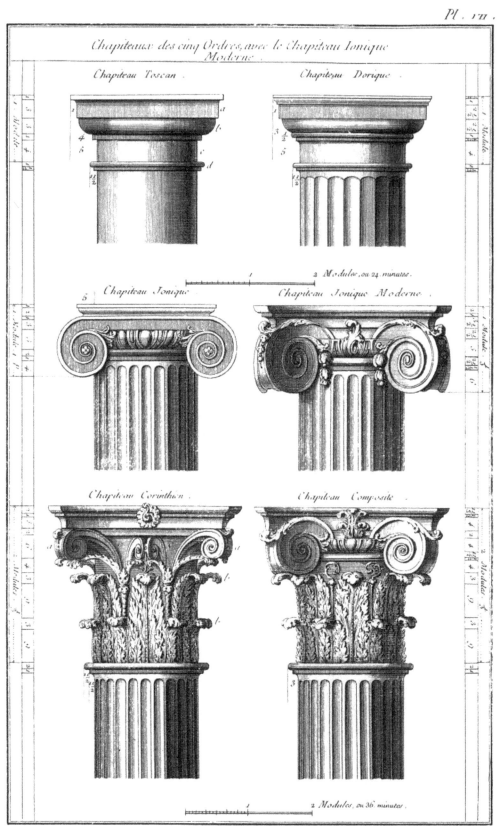

The five orders of architecture compared, showing two versions of the Ionic Order

In fact the seven liberal arts and sciences had been codified many centuries earlier. In the year ad 819, Archbishop Rabanus Maurus of Mainz defined them in the following manner:

> ***Grammar*** *is the science which teaches us to explain the poets and historians; it is the art which qualifies us to write and speak correctly.* ***Rhetoric*** *is the art of using secular discourse effectively in the circumstances of daily life.* ***Dialectic*** *[logic] is the science of the understanding, which fits us for investigations and definitions, for explanations, and for distinguishing the true from the false.* ***Arithmetic*** *is the science of pure extension determinable by numbers. Ignorance of numbers leaves many things unintelligible.* ***Geometry*** *is an exposition of form proceeding from observation. For every excellent and well-ordered arrangement can be reduced to the special requirements of this science.* ***Music*** *is the science of time intervals as they are perceived by tones. Pythagoras testifies that this world was created by music, and can be ruled by it; thus it is possible that to him, who does not know even a little music, many things remain closed and hidden.* ***Astronomy***, *of which we now speak, teaches the laws of the stellar world ...which is built up on the investigation of natural phenomena in order to determine the course of the sun, of the moon, and the stars, and to effect a proper reckoning of time.*

Compare that with the definitions laid down in the fourth section of the second Emulation lecture:

> ***Grammar*** *teaches the proper arrangement of words ... and that excellence of pronunciation which enable us to speak and write a language with accuracy and precision, agreeably to reason, authority, and the strict rules of literature.* ***Rhetoric*** *teaches us to speak copiously and fluently on any subject ... with all the advantages of force and elegance ...* ***Logic*** *teaches us to guide our reason ... and to direct our inquiries after truth ... it consists of regular trains of argument whence we infer, deduce and conclude ... in it are employed the faculties of conceiving, reasoning, judging and disposing ...* ***Arithmetic*** *teaches the powers and properties of numbers ... by this art, reasons and demonstrations are given for finding any certain number whose relation ... to another number is already discovered.* ***Geometry*** *treats of the powers and properties of magnitude in general where length, length and breadth, or length, breadth and thickness are considered ...* ***Music*** *teaches us the art of forming concords, so as to produce a delightful harmony ... it enquires into the nature of concords and discords and enables us to find out a due proportion between them ...* ***Astronomy*** *is that divine art by which we are taught to read the wisdom, strength and beauty of the Almighty Creator in the sacred pages of the celestial hemisphere ... by it also we learn the ... primary laws of nature; and while we are employed in the study of this science, we may perceive unparalleled instances of wisdom and goodness ...*

In the 21st century, it is interesting to note how a prominent author, Michael Baigent, views the liberal arts and sciences from a Masonic point of view:

Grammar teaches us to understand the writings of others in order that we may learn. *Rhetoric* concerns the skill of effective expression in order that we may persuade and teach. *Logic* gives us the ability to investigate and understand what we experience. *Arithmetic* is the science of numbers, *Geometry* of measurement and form; *Music* teaches of time, tones and rhythm – these three all concern the harmony and proportion of the created world; they concern the multitude of forms which emanate from the One divine source – which we call the Great Architect of the Universe. And, *Astronomy* leads us into contemplation of the heavens that we might consider the infinite works of the Great Architect.

The remarkable thing is, that although these definitions, separated by more than eleven hundred years, have different approaches to the subject matter, their central ideas are the same. If we sum them up, we can see now how men, particularly Freemasons, in the Age of Enlightenment, were keen to employ all their intellectual powers, not only in solving material problems, but also in the pursuit of the intellectual and spiritual quests of their day. The real search for truth, and the striving for progress, had begun in earnest.

THE THIRD DEGREE

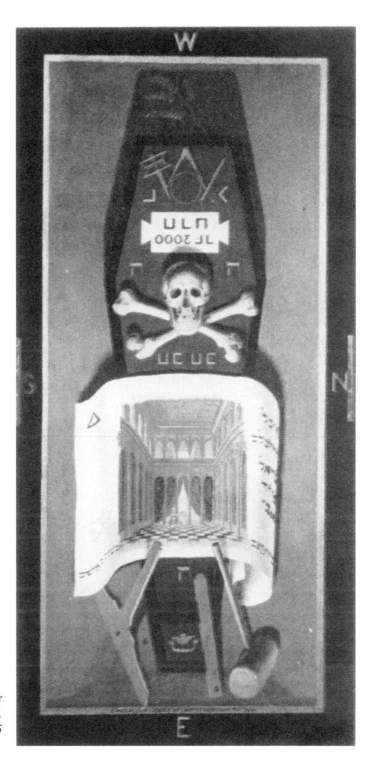

*Emulation third degree
tracing board,
John Harris 1845*

Death be not proud, though some have called thee
Mighty and dreadfull, for thou art not so,
For those whom thou think'st thou dost overthrow
Die not, poore death, nor yet canst thou kill me.
From rest and sleepe, which but thy pictures bee,
Much pleasure then from thee, much more must flow,
And soonest our best men with thee doe goe,
Rest of their bones, and soules deliverie.
Thou art slave to Fate, Chance, kings, and desperate men,
And dost with poyson, warre, and sicknesse dwell,
And poppie, or charmes can make us sleepe as well,
And better than thy stroake; why swell'st thou then;
One short sleepe past, wee wake eternally,
And death shall be no more; death, thou shalt die.

John Donne, 1572-1631

This little poem by one of the finest lyric poets of the 17th century, reminds us what the third degree in Freemasonry is about. It is not quite correct to say that the third degree is about death – it is rather about man's triumph over death, and that on two levels. On one level, in the third degree legend, we bury the old, unregenerated self, in order to ascend to a new perfected state, to 'lift our eyes to that bright morning star, whose rising brings peace and salvation to the faithful and obedient of the human race'. And the second level of course flows from that: it is an assertion that, with God's aid, we can attain to life everlasting, an experience of eternity, that the vital and immortal principle, which is our own spirit, will pass through the mysterious veil which the eye of human reason cannot penetrate 'unless assisted by that Light which is from above'. Let us remember this when studying the symbols of the tracing board of the sublime degree in Freemasonry.

CONTENTS OF THE BOARD

As in the previous degrees, let us first examine the individual items on the board. This board is simpler than the other two – there are fewer objects, but their import is in many ways deeper than those of the other two boards. Dominating the design is the coffin, drawn as a three-dimensional object, so we can see the outside of the head of the coffin, where a sprig of acacia lies. At the foot of the coffin are arranged the three implements with which, we are told, Hiram Abiff was slain, namely the plumb rule, level and heavy maul.

The majority of the objects and inscriptions seem to rest on the close-fitting lid of the coffin. At the head we see the working tools of a Master Mason, which are, from left to right, the skirret, compasses and pencil, with a circle described between the legs of the compasses. But on either side of these are two shapes – on the left what looks like the mirror image of the letter L, and on the right a right-angle whose arms point north east and south east. For an elucidation of these, as well as other similar symbols on this board, we must understand a little about Masonic cypher.

DECODING

John Harris, who designed the three boards we are considering in detail, adapted a cypher, the form of which is shown below. This Masonic cypher, and variations of it, have been in use for many years. It can be used either logically, from left to right, or to render it more incomprehensible, from right to left. Thus there are two forms, the second form a mirror image of the first. Once we understand this, the two characters either side of the working tools can be interpreted, reading from right to left, as TC – Tubal Cain. Below these, on what appears to be an inscribed metal plate, are the letters, again from right to left, HAB – Hiram Abiff, and still reading in the same direction, AL 3000 – Anno Lucis 3000, the year of Hiram's death.

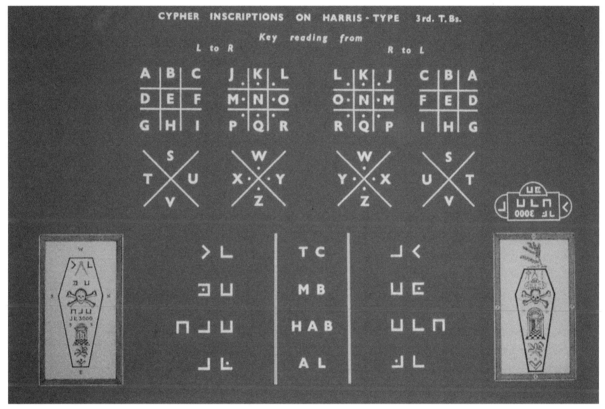

Masonic cypher adapted by John Harris

Below that inscribed plate are the skull and crossbones, to either side of which at the top is the Hebrew character ה or Hē which, being the fifth letter of the Hebrew alphabet, denotes the number five. This character is repeated at the foot of the coffin on the lid, just by the plumb rule. Beneath the skull and cross bones we see the letters MB twice.

THE DEATH OF HIRAM ABIFF

Just as, in the second degree, much important information has been left out of the symbolism of the tracing board of that degree, so in this degree there is nothing on the board that relates to the actual death of Hiram Abiff. The only information that the board gives us relates to the events subsequent to his death. But as we see when we study the ritual, there are some crucial aspects of the third degree, aspects of the death of Hiram, which are not represented on the tracing board.

In the ritual we find the first and perhaps greatest lesson taught by the legend. Death, we are told, is to be reflected upon. The objects of the third degree

> *... teach you to feel that, to the just and virtuous man, death has no terrors equal to the stain of falsehood and dishonour.*

There then follows the legendary account of the death of Hiram Abiff, who was slain just before the completion of King Solomon's temple. The legend recounts how fifteen Fellow Crafts were envious of those who had the secrets of a Master Mason, believing no doubt that possession of those secrets would confer on them advancement in either status or material wealth. Twelve retracted, but three persisted, and ambushed Hiram in the temple itself. His reply to the demands that he should betray those secrets has an important moral message for us. When challenged to divulge the secrets under pain of death, he replied that

> *... those secrets were known to but three in the world, and that without the consent and cooperation of the other two, he neither could nor would divulge them, but intimated that he had no doubt patience and industry would, in due time, entitle the worthy Mason to a participation of them, but that, for his own part, he would rather suffer death than betray the sacred trust reposed in him.*

As we know, this defence by Hiram in his determination not to disclose the secrets was to no avail, and events moved inexorably towards his assassination. The legend of his death carries an important lesson for us. The heavy maul or mall, used in conjunction with the chisel, is an emblem of creativity. The level is an emblem of equality implying that, however highly qualified, the three original Grand Masters cannot claim superiority in virtue or intellect over these Fellow Crafts. The plumb rule, the ultimate emblem of uprightness and integrity, when placed in the hands of the true craftsman, leads him to unfailing goodness in his dealings with his fellow men. But envy, the all-consuming passion of those who killed Hiram, led to a corruption, a distortion of the true import of these working tools. In their actions, there was no creativity, rather destruction. There was no virtue in the equality they aspired to. And there was no integrity in their actions. As Kirk MacNulty puts it in *The Way of the Craftsman* 'The symbolism suggests that the process has to do with the effect of wilfulness and uncontrolled passion, where truth and integrity should be found.' The moral for us is a powerful one.

In the ceremony of the third degree, the Master later reminds us that Hiram

> *... lost his life in consequence of his unshaken fidelity to the sacred trust reposed in him, and I hope this will make a lasting impression on his and your minds should you ever be placed in a similar state of trial.*

We have therefore a further moral of the importance of faithfulness to a trust placed in us as human beings and particularly as Freemasons.

A CHARGE

The candidate is then raised up, following which the Master addresses him with the Charge after raising, which must surely count as one of the most beautiful passages in Masonic ritual. The Master exhorts the candidate to

> *... observe that the light of a Master Mason is darkness visible ...*

We spoke earlier about changes of perspective, and here we meet one of the most baffling. How, we may ask ourselves, can light be darkness, and how can darkness be visible? We may consider that to see in darkness requires different talents, heightened perceptions and highly developed skills. A blind person, for example, often senses moods and movements around him because, lacking the sense of sight, his other senses are better developed and he is thereby able to 'see' some things better than a sighted person. So it is here, when we are seeking knowledge of ourselves, and insights into human nature in general. The 18th century writer and poet Alexander Pope referred to this paradox, and in doing so, illustrated rather well the need to look beyond the obvious:

> *Of darkness visible so much be lent,*
> *As half to shew, half veil the deep Intent.*

The ritual continues:

> *... the light of a Master Mason is darkness visible, serving only to express that gloom which rests on the prospect of futurity.*

In 21st century English, 'to express' is to make clear or expand on. We should note here the 18th century meaning of' 'to express' as meaning 'to push out', 'to dispel', so the darkness visible, the gift of a Master Mason, enables us to dispel any negative influences, or 'gloom', which we may sense approaching up ahead in our lives.

THROUGH THE VEIL

The Master continues:

> *It is that mysterious veil which the eye of human reason cannot penetrate, unless assisted by that Light which is from above.*

So although the ethos of Freemasonry is firmly rooted in the Age of Reason, the Age of Enlightenment, the supremacy of the Great Architect is firmly acknowledged, leaving human reason, invaluable though it is, in second place to the power of the Almighty to save and heal humankind.

> *Let the emblems of mortality which lie before you lead you to contemplate on your inevitable destiny, and guide your reflections to that most interesting of all human studies, the knowledge of yourself.*

The journey towards self-knowledge, which began with the blindfold in the first degree, has now come full circle, to the point where, in contemplation of the apparent finality of death, we can learn to know ourselves as heirs to immortality, the dazzling brightness, the blazing star or glory, rather than the gloom of futurity.

> *Continue to listen to the voice of nature, which bears witness that, even in this perishable frame, resides a vital and immortal principle, which inspires a holy confidence that the Lord of Life will enable us to trample the King of Terrors beneath our feet, and lift our eyes to that bright Morning Star, whose rising brings peace and salvation to the faithful and obedient of the human race.*

Having learned to know ourselves, discovered our own vital and immortal principle, namely the spark of divinity within ourselves, we can indeed ensure the triumph of good over evil.

Appropriate to this point of the third degree ceremony are the words of Neville Barker Cryer. He responded to a question put to him by the writer in the following words:

We can appreciate what is said in the catechism of the third degree opening. 'What inducement have you to leave the east and go to the west?' 'To seek for that which was lost, which, by your instruction and our own industry, we hope to find' 'What is that which was lost?' 'The genuine secrets of a Master Mason.' What this clearly means is that the candidate for the true degree of Master Mason was to pass from the east, between the two pillars, recognising what lay at the top of the ladder of Jacob, through the Holy Place where stood the door of the Holy of Holies in the west to the Ark of the Covenant, where he would discover the very name and presence of God. It is also interesting that a word used amongst the Jews as an alternative to pronouncing the name of God is the word that we translate as 'heaven'. We can now see the full meaning of the phrase in the opening ceremony of the third degree ' ... may heaven aid our united endeavours.' God is being requested to assist the Masters, or principals, of the Lodge to unite in leading this candidate for Mastership to reach the goal of his Masonry.

TRADITIONAL HISTORY

As far as the Emulation ritual is concerned, the main features of the board are explained by means of the traditional history. This portion of the ceremony of raising to the third or sublime degree of Master Mason relates the legendary events following the death of the principal architect of King Solomon's temple. We were informed, in the second degree, that 'three rule a Lodge', and that Hiram Abiff was the third of the three Grand Masters who bore sway at the building of the temple. When King Solomon was made aware of the unexplained absence of Hiram Abiff he selected fifteen Fellow Crafts to go out and search for their missing Master. These fifteen formed themselves into three Lodges, thus forming three groups of five, and this number is indicated on the lid of the coffin by the three Hebrew characters ה or 'Hē' alluded to earlier.

The searches of the first group were fruitless, and they returned to Jerusalem. The second group discovered the hastily buried body of Hiram Abiff in a badly concealed grave. Before returning to Jerusalem to inform King Solomon of their discovery, they marked the spot where the body was buried with a sprig of acacia, a plant that has become identified with Freemasonry in general, but particularly as a symbol of mourning.

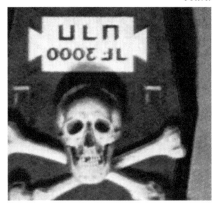

Detail of Emulation third degree tracing board

THE TRACING BOARD

After the progress of the three groups of five Fellow Crafts has been dealt with, the Master now explains features of the board to the candidate.

> *Our Master was ordered to be reinterred as near to the Sanctum Sanctorum*
> *as the Israelitish law would permit; there in a grave from the centre three*
> *feet east and three feet west, three feet between north and south, and five*
> *feet or more perpendicular.*

The Emulation Lodge of Improvement boards are indeed approximately 183 cm (6 ft) by 91 cm (3 ft) but these dimensions are significant for another reason. If we regard the candidate as having been raised from a figurative death to a reunion with the former companions of his toils, then the grave is an image of his unregenerated self The lost guiding light represents his vital and immortal principle, physically delineated by three feet, or an arm's length, in each direction, and five feet or more, his own height, perpendicular, an allegory of his own body.

> *He was not buried in the Sanctum Sanctorum because nothing common*
> *or unclean was allowed to enter there, not even the High Priest but once*
> *a year, nor then until after many washings and purifications against the*
> *great day of expiation for sins, for by the Israelitish law all flesh was deemed*
> *unclean. The same fifteen trusty Fellow Crafts were ordered to attend the*
> *funeral, clothed in white aprons and gloves as emblems of their innocence.*

So here the insistence by the temple authorities on purity and nobility of spirit is answered by King Solomon in ensuring that his men were clothed in emblems of purity and innocence, emblems that we as Freemasons adhere to today, in the form of white aprons and white gloves.

On the scroll lying across the coffin is a picture depicting the ornaments of a Master Mason's Lodge, which are

> *... the porch, dormer and square pavement. The porch was the entrance*
> *to the Sanctum Sanctorum; the dormer the window that gave light to the*
> *same; and the square pavement for the High Priest to walk on.*

We mentioned the ornaments in the first degree: the mosaic pavement, the blazing star, and the indented or tesselated border. Here in the third degree, the allegorical references are striking. The candidate enters the Sanctum Sanctorum by the porch, just as in the second degree he entered the middle chamber by the door. So the porch is here the transition point of his passage from the second to the third degree. Once in the Holy Place, the light flooding in through the dormer becomes the blazing star or glory in the centre of the first degree, namely the omnipresence of God. But the ornament which is common to all three degrees is the mosaic or square pavement. In this degree however, unlike in the other two, the square pavement is 'for the High Priest to walk on', not for any mere mortal, but since the candidate is now raised from his old unregenerated self to greater purity, he has become qualified to tread on the square pavement in the company of the High Priest himself.

The only remaining objects to detail on the scroll are the Hebrew inscriptions to left and right of the picture of the ornaments, the triangle at top left and the faintly drawn pentalpha lower down. The Hebrew inscriptions may be reconstructed as follows, but only the words in italics are visible:

At the right of the scroll The *Temple of Jerusalem* was built by Solomon King of *Israel*, Hiram King of *Tyre* and Hiram *Abi*(f) in the year 2992

At the left foot of scroll *In the year 3 thousands*

For the full inscription, see the explanation on page 57 in the next chapter.

The triangle seems to refer to the three original Grand Masters, and the pentalpha relates to the five points of fellowship. The interlacing in this way of the five legs of the star gives an added brightness and understanding to the almost mystical nature of this Masonic symbol. Indeed, the five points of fellowship are the most sublime reference anywhere in Masonic ritual to the mutuality of brotherhood in Freemasonry.

Situated at the very top of the coffin lid, directly beneath the sprig of acacia, are the working tools of a Master Mason, and the Master concludes the degree ceremony with an explanation of them. The working tools of the first degree, twenty-four-inch gauge, gavel and chisel, were tools of action. The second degree tools were tools of testing – the square, level and plumb rule. In the third degree, the working tools are tools of creativity – the pencil translates into tangible form the inner vision of the artist, his creative force, and the skirret sets the limits of the pencil, should that be necessary. But the compasses act as a balancing influence between the two, and circumscribe our actions and our existence, reminding us of God's impartial justice, who

> ... *having defined for our instruction the limits of good and evil, will reward, or punish, as we have obeyed, or disregarded, His divine commands.*

A LITTLE HISTORY
AND SOME VARIATIONS

For a comprehensive and detailed account of how tracing boards came to be used in Lodges, the definitive work is *Tracing Boards – Their Development and Their Designers* by Terence O. Haunch, published by the Quatuor Coronati Correspondence Circle. We will not attempt to reproduce that here, but we will cover the subject in broad outline.

Terence Haunch says that in the days when the primitive operative Lodge met out of doors, the marking out of a ritual enclosure on the ground was a familiar and explainable practice. It is easy to see how this came to be called 'the Lodge' and when meetings were later held indoors, such a marking out came to be identified with the Lodge as an entity. The marking out was then in the form of 'an oblong square', the rectangle or double square we have become accustomed to. We mentioned earlier, in the section explaining the first degree board, how the form of the Lodge is a double cube, being as high as it is broad, and twice as long. This double cube signifies the proximity of the celestial and terrestrial realms, and their one-ness when joined.

That this symbolical 'Lodge' came to be codified and embellished to become what we today recognise as a tracing board, in itself such a rectangle, is not hard to imagine. The 'Lodge', namely that drawing which depicted, early on,

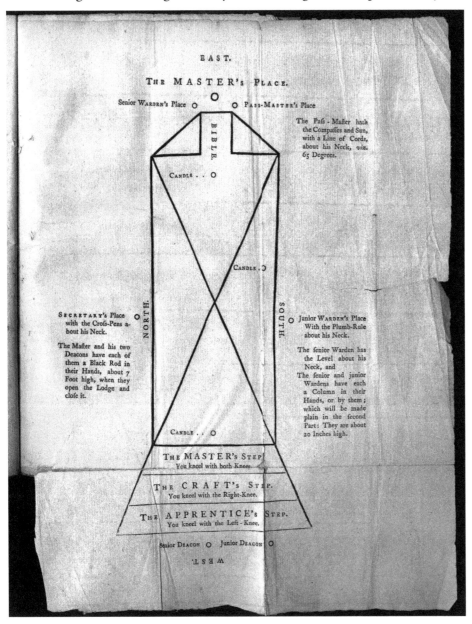

Drawing from Three Distinct Knocks

the symbols for the study of the Brethren in Craft Freemasonry, seems to have been as important, if not more so, than the physical building in which they held their assemblies, or the idea of the 'Lodge' as consisting of the Brethren themselves gathered together.

As with many things in Masonic history, the earliest references to 'drawing the Lodge' come to us through exposures. In 1760, one such exposure called *Three Distinct Knocks*, gave the drawing we show opposite, which is little more than a line-sketch.

Frontispiece of
Mahhabone

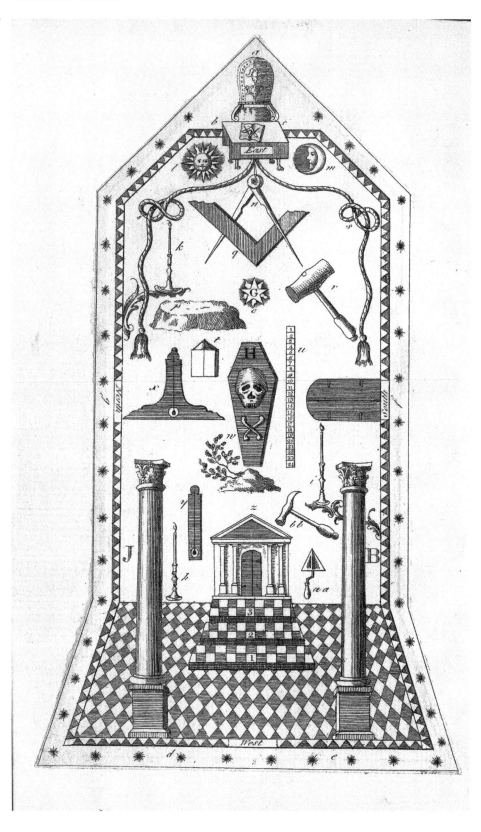

The 'Drawing on the Floor of a Lodge' on the previous page, which forms the frontispiece of another exposure *Mahhabone* published in 1766, copies the overall shape of this sketch, while embellishing it with symbols which we would recognise on today's boards. This plan owes at least two of its features to lodge cloths in use in France at the period: the 'pointed cubic stone' in place of the perfect ashlar, and the 'indented tuft' or ornamental tassel affixed to a cord. We shall see more of these in the next chapter.

By this time the designs were being reproduced on floor cloths, as it was becoming too laborious to rub out or

EXPLANATION.

1 First Degree, or Entered Apprentice's Step.---2 Second Degree, or Fellow Craft's Step.---3 Third Degree, or Master's Step.---*a* Master's Chair, wherein he fits to open the Lodge, with the Rule, Compass, and Square; also a Table, whereon is laid a Bible open, with the Square and Compass across, and himself properly vested, with a black Rod in his Hand near seven Feet high.---*b* Senior Deacon, with the Compass, and a black Rod in his Hand.---*c* A Pass'd Master, with the Sun and Compass, and a String of Cords.---*d* Senior Warden, with the Level, and a Column in his Hand about twenty Inches long.---*e* Junior Deacon, with the Compass, and a black Rod in his Hand.---*f* Junior Warden, with the Plumb Rule, and a Column in his Hand, at the Entrance of the South Gate.---*g* Secretary, with Cross-pens.---*h i k* Three Candles, fix'd triangular.---*l* The Sun.---*m* The Moon.---*n* The Compass.---*o* The Blazing Star.---*p* The rough Stone.---*q* The Square.---*r* The Mallet.---*s* The indented Tuft.---*t* The pointed cubical Stone.---*u* The twenty-four Inch Guage.---*w* The Coffin of *Hiram*, with the Sprig of *Acacia*.---*x* The Level.---*y* The Plumb-rule.---*z* The Western Porch.---*aa* The Trowel.---*bb* The Common Gavel.---J B The two Columns called *Jachin* and *Boaz*.--- ✳ Members standing round at the Ceremony of Making.

The Uses of the above Materials are fully defined in the Course of the Work, both spiritually and temporally.

wash away the design every time the Lodge was closed. These practices were being copied on the continent, in France in the form of 'tapis de la loge' or lodge cloths or carpets, and in Germany and Austria as 'Logentapis'. A later exposure showed a French Lodge at work, and this was reproduced in England by a printer, Thomas Palser, as shown at the foot of this page, showing the Brethren ranged on either side of a floor cloth with symbols depicted on it.

To quote the work of Terence Haunch mentioned earlier, as these artefacts were becoming more elaborate and requiring some artistic skill they had become expensive, and 'the desire would arise to prevent them from defacement on

18th century depiction of an initiation, engraving by Thomas Palser

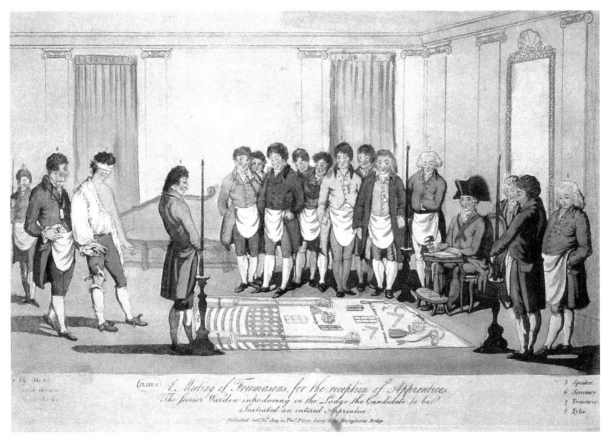

the floor. It would then seem a natural thing to drape the cloth over a table, to support it on a board or trestles, or to hang it on the wall on rollers.'

There could, says Haunch, be no objection to this. The primitive significance of the drawing as the 'form of the lodge', a representation of that symbolical enclosure within which certain ritual practices must take place, had become only a vague tradition, not properly understood, if remembered at all. It would then be only a short step to supporting the floor cloth on a table, or executing the design on some rigid frame such as a board, which would then either be laid on the floor or supported on trestles.

There is some evidence that the term 'trestle board', 'trassle board' and other variants became corrupted into 'traising board' and later 'tracing board' or in France, 'planche à tracer'. In the USA the term 'trestle board' is still used for this object, although it is also used, in a figurative sense, as a term for a programme of work, or for a lecture.

EARLY DESIGNERS

Some of the earliest floor cloths and boards contained symbols of all three degrees, but gradually separate boards, one for each degree, came to be used. The various designs produced were often arbitrary, depicting the symbols of the degree according to the fancy of the individual designer. Very few of these dating from before 1800 have survived, but after that year the names of certain designers come to the fore. One of the earliest was John Cole, whose engravings for a full set of three boards appeared in 1801. His designs follow what Terence Haunch calls the 'Masonic chart pattern', and they do not show evidence of great aesthetic merit or artistic aspirations, merely laying out the symbols in a more or less arbitrary way.

We should note in the first degree board the key, and the different heights of the pillars, which accord with the actual architectural specification, that the Doric pillar is seven diameters high, the Ionic eight, and the Corinthian nine. Here the Doric pillar is called wisdom and the Ionic strength, as was the practice before the Union in 1813.

Tracing boards designed by John Cole

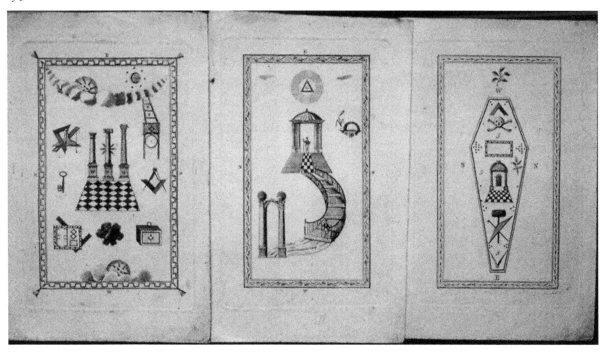

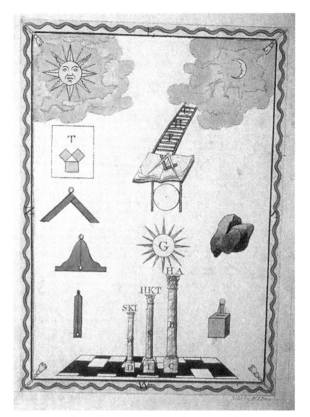

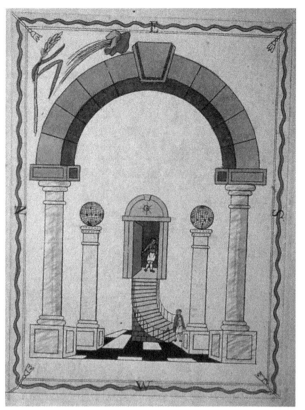

Note also the diagonal chequered pavement, the Greek key border, the blazing star partly hidden by the Ionic pillar, and the sun, both rising in the east and setting in the west. In the second degree board the staircase, approached between the pillars, winds from the north side, and in the third degree the working tools are the heavy beetle, another name for a maul or mall, the setting level and the plotting pin.

Tracing boards designed by John Browne

A contemporary of Cole, John Browne, produced in about 1800 designs which began to move away from the 'Masonic chart' treatment towards more subtle, aesthetically pleasing designs, rendered in colour.

Browne is more widely known for his cypher ritual, which was published under the title *Master Key*. On Browne's first degree board the Doric pillar, in agreement with Cole, alludes to Solomon King of Israel and the Ionic pillar to Hiram King of Tyre. On the second degree board, the staircase winds from the south but the board shows the entrance to the middle chamber directly between the two pillars. The third degree board has some interesting features. The three Lodges of five Fellow Crafts are shown by three files of bees; in the top file the fifth bee is represented by the craftsman pulling a shrub from the ground. In 18th century Freemasonry, bees and beehives were much in use as emblems of industry, an emblem still used today in Freemasonry in other countries. The monogram lower right is a composite of the initials of Solomon King of Israel, Hiram King of Tyre and Hiram Abiff. Note also that all three boards feature the tassels at the four corners of the boards – nowadays these only appear on the first degree board.

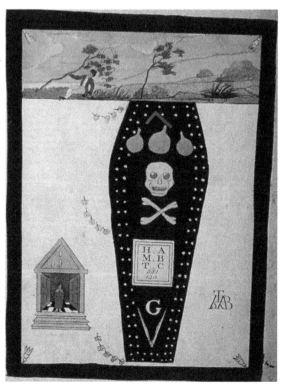

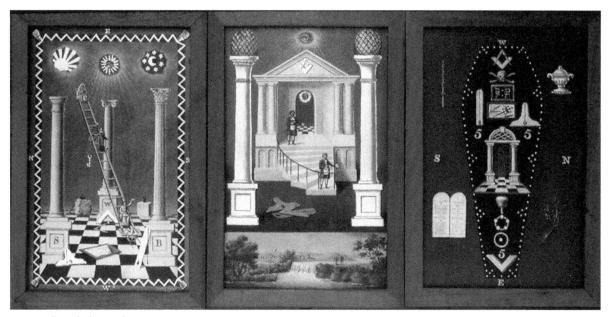

Tracing boards designed by Josiah Bowring for the Lodge of Honor and Generosity

With the advent of boards designed by Josiah Bowring, still dating from before the Union of the two Grand Lodges in 1813, a new dimension was added to the tracing boards being produced in the early 19th century. Bowring was a portrait painter, and his boards show greater artistic merit than those designed up to his time. For the first time, the Christian virtues on Jacob's Ladder are represented as female figures and not merely by the letters F, H and C. The indented or tesselated border looks more like the present-day feature, and the pillars now agree with present-day practice, namely Ionic alluding to wisdom, Doric to strength and Corinthian to beauty.

In the first Bowring board, at the foot of the ladder, can be seen the three Great Lights and the two grand parallel lines either side of the point within a circle. The key hanging from the ladder refers to the first section of the first Emulation lecture, when speaking of secrets.

Q. As Masons, how do we hope to get at them?

A. By the help of a key.

Q. Does that key hang or lie?

A. It hangs.

Q. Why is the preference given to hanging?

A. It should always hang in a Brother's defence, and never lie to his prejudice

Q. What does it hang by?

A. The thread of life, in the passage of utterance, between guttural and pectoral.

Q. Why so nearly connected with the heart?

A. Being an index of the mind, it should utter nothing but what the heart truly dictates.

Q. It is a curious key; of what metal is it composed?

A. No metal; it is the tongue of good report.

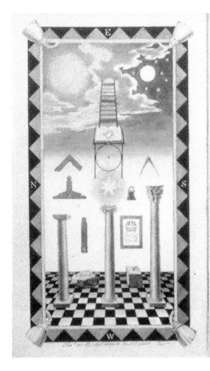
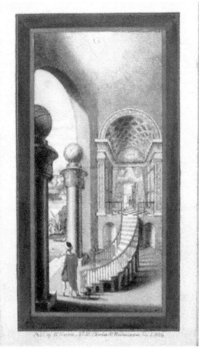
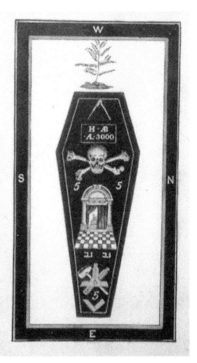

John Harris set of boards
from 1820

A NEW STAR RISING

In the words of Terence Haunch, all these designers 'were soon to be overshadowed by one whose name became inseparably linked in the nineteenth century with the design of tracing boards'. John Harris was a painter of miniatures, architectural draughtsman and facsimilist – all qualities which fitted him to become an outstanding designer of tracing boards. He first published a set of boards, sold as sets of cards approximately 33 cm (9 in.) by 13 cm (5 in.) in 1820. His first degree board owes much to the chart pattern of earlier designers, with little perspective. The ladder, three Great Lights and the point within a circle with the parallel lines all appear to be somewhat removed from the other emblems. The ladder is not as prominent as on the Bowring board, but interestingly he depicts the lewis separately, and the blazing star, logically and in conformity with the wording of the lecture, is near the middle of the board. There is no mention of the Christian virtues of faith, hope and charity, and the key has not been included, but the tassels are the most prominent we have seen up to this date.

The second degree board shows a view of King Solomon's temple which is more simple than the one we are used to today, but is also confused. The two great pillars are shown, not at the east entrance, but at the south porchway leading to the foot of the staircase. However, this board is a great improvement over the first degree board in terms of perspective, and the blazing star or glory is shown in the ceiling of the porch.

The pictorial message of the third degree board is simple and direct. Harris only uses the mirror image of the cypher for the letters MB, shown twice; there is no mention of Tubal Cain and the references to Hiram Abiff and the year of his death are also shown uncoded.

John Harris's 1825 set of boards show some important evolution. There is more cohesion between the elements composing the designs. Here, in the first board, the working tools, the movable and immovable jewels and the ashlars are disposed in a way that links their symbolism. The blazing star or glory has

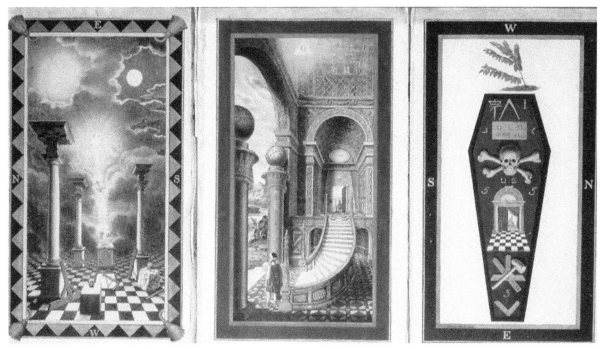

*John Harris set of boards
from 1825*

been placed at the head of the ladder, adding meaning to its symbolism, and the three Christian virtues on the ladder are represented by symbols, a chalice, an anchor and a woman and child. The mosaic pavement stretches back into the background as an indirect indication of eternity. In the second board Harris still has the pillars, wrongly, at the south porchway. The third board shows the Tubal Cain initials in mirror-image code, shows all the working tools – only one was shown in the 1820 board – and has the initials MB in mirror-image code.

In 1845 the Emulation Lodge of Improvement launched a competition for an improvement in tracing boards. The competition was won by John Harris, whose boards, painted in the same year, are those which have been in use by the Lodge from that day to the present. These boards are approximately 183 cm (6 ft) by 91 cm (3 ft) and are displayed, on trestles, in the middle of the floor at all meetings of the Lodge on Friday evenings at Freemasons' Hall, London, from October to June each year. Their success was immediate, and they are now the most widely used boards in England, even in those Lodges which do not work the Emulation ritual.

By comparison with Harris's 1825 boards, the first degree board has a far more pronounced perspective. The Christian virtues have been replaced by human figures, the perfect ashlar is supported by a derrick, figures depicting Solomon King of Israel, Hiram King of Tyre and Hiram Abiff have been placed on the tops of the pillars, the clouds of 1825 have disappeared and the tesselated border is more finely-drawn.

In the second degree board Harris appears to have rectified the mistake of showing the two great pillars as flanking the porchway on the south side. Here, he has split the board to show us a vista of the main temple looking through the east entrance past the pillars – a very impressive view, owing nothing to any second degree board published up to that time. The south porchway with the winding staircase is now shown, with no pillars, in the top one-third portion of the board, with the mosaic pavement arranged diagonally.

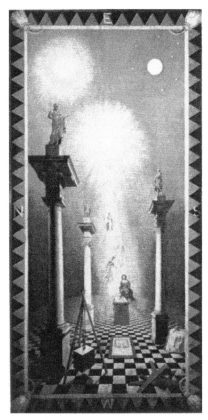
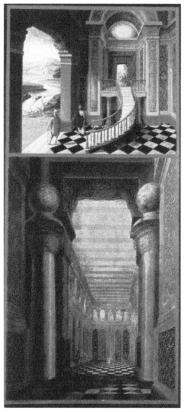
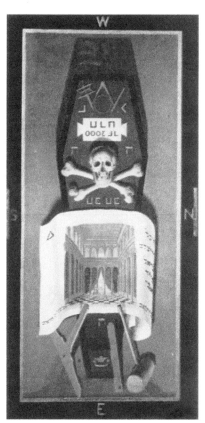

FIRST DEGREE   SECOND DEGREE   THIRD DEGREE

The third board shows some marked improvements. Harris has here introduced some perspective – the coffin is now clearly a three-dimensional object, and the scroll we referred to in Chapter 3 on the third degree has been introduced as a means of illustrating the ornaments of a Master Mason's Lodge. The letters MB are repeated, and the numerals 5, repeated three times and denoting the three Fellow Crafts' Lodges, are represented by the Hebrew letter ה or Hē which, being the fifth letter of the Hebrew alphabet, denotes the number five.

Above: John Harris boards designed for the Emulation Lodge of Improvement in 1845.

Below: John Harris set of boards from 1849

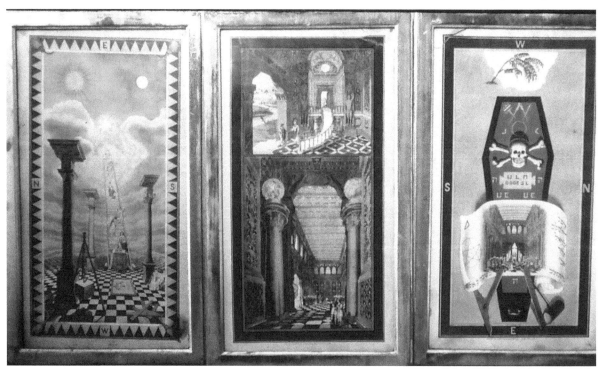

Third degree tracing board designed by John Harris in 1849/50

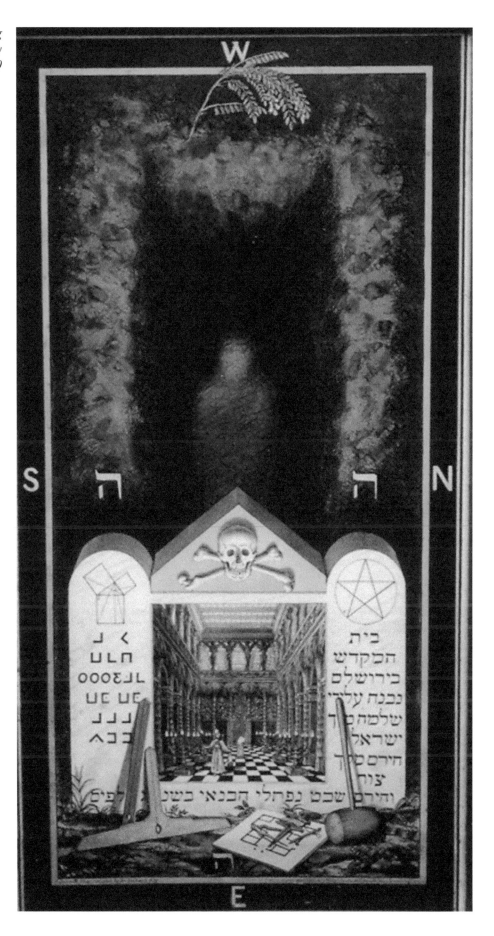

Although the 1845 set of boards became the 'official' boards of the Emulation Lodge of Improvement, Harris designed, in 1849, a further set. In the first degree board of this set, the figures atop the pillars have disappeared, the clouds have returned, and the blazing star or glory is removed from the top of the ladder to a position higher in the sky. In the third board, much of the perspective has been removed but it is in other respects much the same.

It is the second degree board which is of most interest to us. In the top section, the square pavement is no longer simply black and white, but is now a more intricate three-coloured pattern, and the black and white square pavement is relegated to the ground floor. In the lower section, the celestial and terrestrial globes have been highlighted in colour, but the most interesting variation is that Harris has introduced, into the vista on the left-hand or south side, a porchway through which can be seen the foot of a staircase winding to the south. It is impossible not to see this as an attempt to rectify what he portrayed wrongly in the 1845 second degree board. Any reconstruction of King Solomon's Temple shows that the main temple area was flanked, on the outside, by covered courtyards, one to the north and the other to the south. But in the south courtyard at least there was no entrance to the outside, so that Harris's picture, in the top section, of a landscape beyond the porchway, cannot be correct, and the reference in the ritual to 'the porchway or entrance on the south side' must therefore refer to a porchway on the south side *of the main temple area*, giving on to the north side of the courtyard beyond. The staircase therefore would wind, not through 90°, but through 180°, to give access at the top *eastwards* to the middle chamber, so called because it was not on the ground or top floors, but on the middle floor. Harris appears then to have hedged his bets, by continuing to show the south or external entrance in the top section, while introducing the south or internal entrance in the bottom section. We mentioned this anomaly already in Chapter 2.

Tracing boards designed by J.E. Godwin

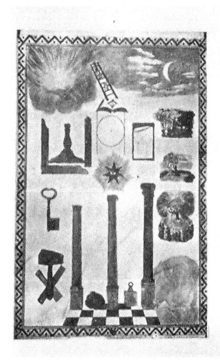
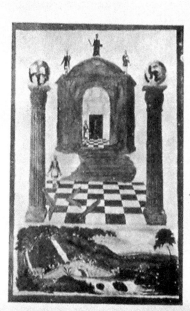
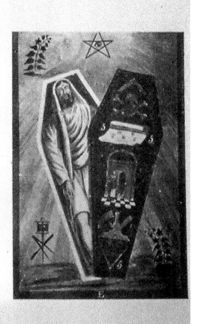

This board was designed by Arthur Thistleton, a London artist, for the Ivanhoe Lodge, Ashby-de-la-Zouch in Leicestershire, in 1836. The Lodge was erased in 1851. Note the maul, twenty-four-inch gauge and lewis arranged above the pillars

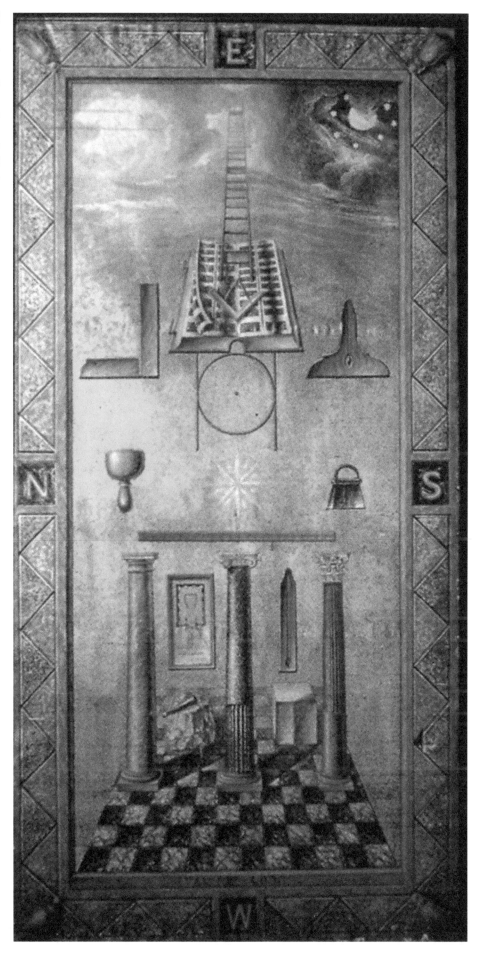

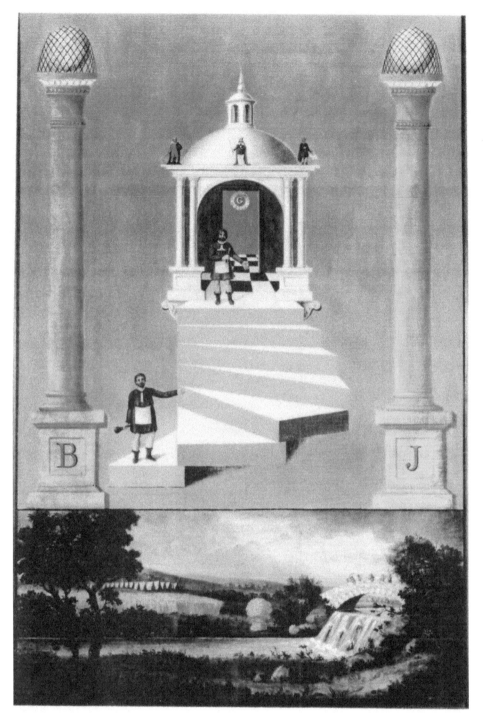

This board belongs to the Lodge of Union, No. 38, and was painted c. 1811 by Josiah Bowring.

The pillars are labelled in the opposite way to present-day practice. The figures on the dome of the middle chamber are those of the three original Grand Masters. The network or canopy is shown very graphically

OTHER BOARDS

For every board designed in England by the best-known and prominent designers of the age, there are many boards of which the provenance is little known, or not known at all. The oldest were in fact not boards at all, but cloths, many of which were later mounted and framed as rigid boards.

Not many boards designed by J.E. Godwin survive. In those published by a Bro. Jacobs, illustrated on page 54, the sun rising and setting is shown, and the virtues on the ladder are depicted by three female figures. On the second board we again see the three original Grand Masters atop the middle chamber. The third degree board shows the skirret as a working tool, a post-Union introduction, so we can be sure these boards date from after 1813. Note the pentalpha here combined with the all-seeing eye.

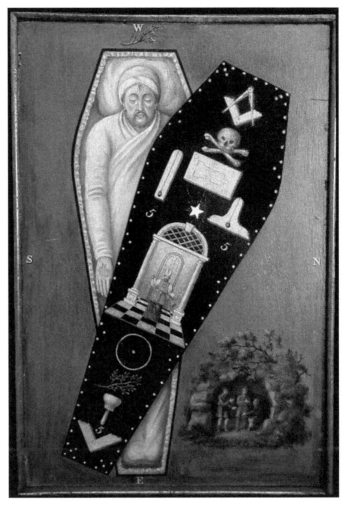

An interesting example of John Harris's work is the third degree board, painted about 1849/50, shown on page 53. The Hebrew inscription is now complete, compared with that on the Emulation Lodge of Improvement board described in Chapter 3 on the third degree. It now reads 'The Holy Temple at Jerusalem was built at the hands of Solomon King of Israel, Hiram King of Tyre and Hiram of the Tribe of Naphtali, the Builder, in the year 3 thousands.' There is a very indistinct view of a shrouded corpse in the bottom of the grave; no coffin is shown. The lines of cypher shown at the left of the scroll are as on the earlier Harris board, with the addition of two lines, reading respectively 'CCC' and 'FFZ', referring to 'chalk charcoal clay' and 'freedom fervency zeal'. These are in allusion to the seventh section of the first Emulation lecture.

Q. How should an Entered Apprentice serve his Master?

A. With freedom, fervency and zeal

Q. Excellent qualities; what are their emblems?

A. Chalk, charcoal and clay

Q. Why?

A. Nothing is more free than chalk; the slightest touch leaves a trace. Nothing more fervent than charcoal, for when properly lighted, no metal can resist its force. Nothing more zealous than clay, our mother earth; she is continually labouring for our support. Thence we came, and there we must all return.

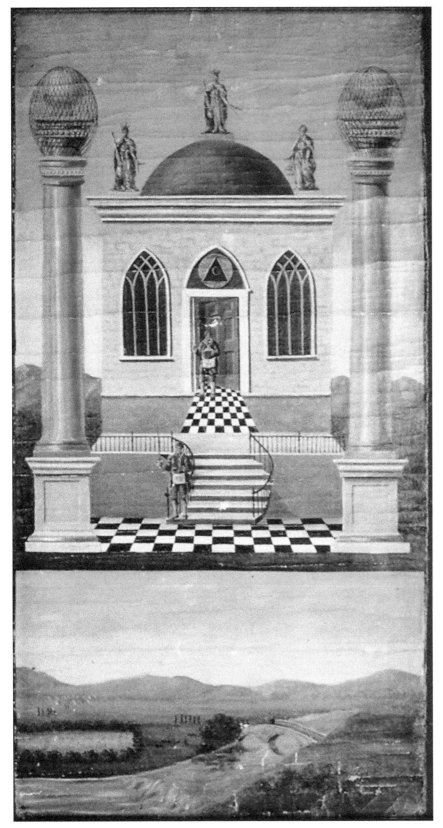

The Lodge in 7th Light Dragoons, No. 262, under the Antients Grand
Lodge, has given us this board, which dates from 1810. This must be one of
the earliest examples of the second degree depiction being divided into two
scenes. The style of the Temple is known as Regency Gothick, and shows the
three original Grand Masters on the dome. The Wardens are wearing their
collar jewels on cords. The crossing of the River Jordan is shown as a bridge
over a waterfall, with a field of corn on the far side.

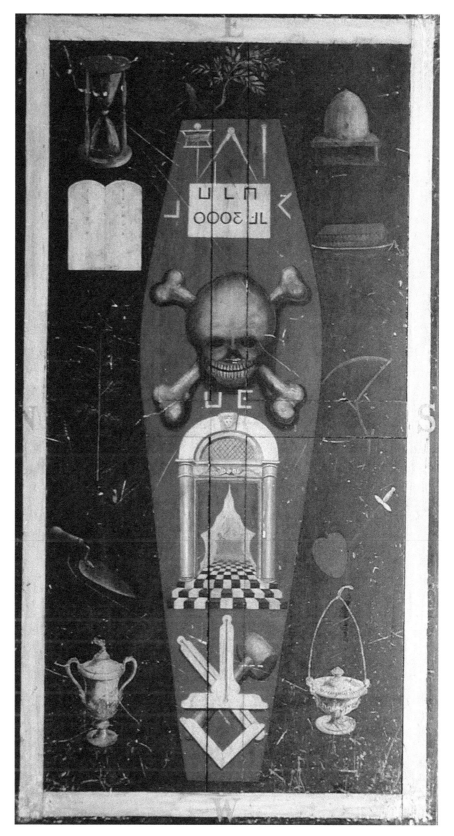

An unusual design of a third degree board was made for the Royal Cumberland Lodge, No. 41, in Bath, Somerset. It exhibits a number of symbols lost to English Craft Masonry after the Union in 1813, but which are retained in the USA. Reading clockwise from the bottom left-hand corner: pot of manna; trowel; Aaron's rod in leaf; tables of the law; hourglass; sprig of acacia; beehive; ark and anchor; scythe; sword pointing at a heart; pot of incense.

The Lodge of Loyalty, No. 86, was consecrated under the Moderns Grand Lodge in 1753. This is their board, age unknown, and the size is approximately 127 cm x 76 cm (50 in. x 30 in.) which makes it one of the larger boards in use in a private Lodge. It is fairly clear that this is based on the *Mahhabone* design on page 45, but with important differences: the cord and the pointed cubic stone shown on the design on page 45 are not shown here, and have never featured on English tracing boards. The first is a feature of lodge boards and lodge cloths in continental Europe, and the second of French Tableaux de Loges; we will see more of these in the next chapter. As in *Mahhabone*, candles are placed east, south and west to represent the three Lesser Lights and there is no perfect ashlar. The common gavel has been replaced by a crow, the trowel seems to have disappeared, and the pillars are not labelled. Like the *Mahhabone* design, there appears to be no reference to the second degree: this board is an amalgam of first and third degree symbolism.

A very interesting set of boards are in the possession of the Phoenix Lodge, No. 94, in Sunderland,

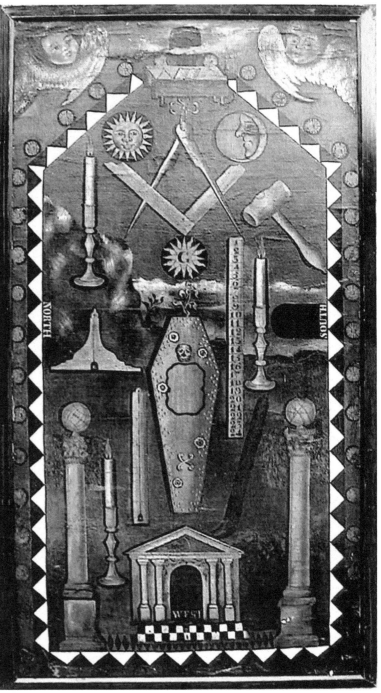

Tracing board of the Lodge of Loyalty

dating from the early 19th century. These are not strictly speaking boards, as they were painted on canvas and were framed at some unknown date to protect them. Note in the first degree board that the all-seeing eye appears in the middle of the clouded canopy right above the Master's tracing board, the first immovable jewel, which is an illustration of a pillared hall, depicting the orders of architecture. The perfect ashlar is shown left supported on a derrick, and the rough ashlar on the right. The five-pointed blazing star is featured underneath the level. There does not appear to be a twenty-four-inch gauge, but a trowel appears to make up the third working tool, while the clock, lower right, is emblematic of the twenty-four hours of the day. There are no tassels, but the four cardinal virtues of Temperance, Fortitude, Prudence and Justice are indicated by their initials. The letters H and G stand for 'Holy Ground', a reference to the fourth section of the first lecture:

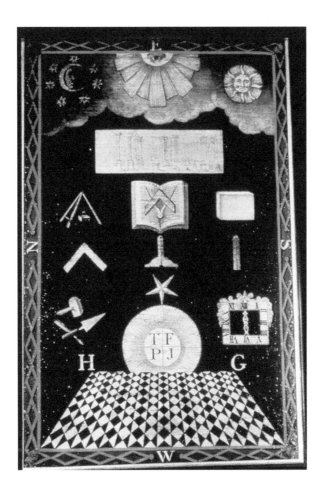

*Tracing boards of the
Phoenix Lodge*

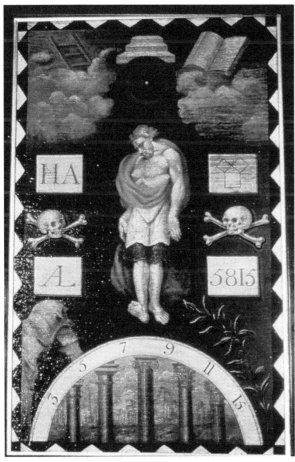

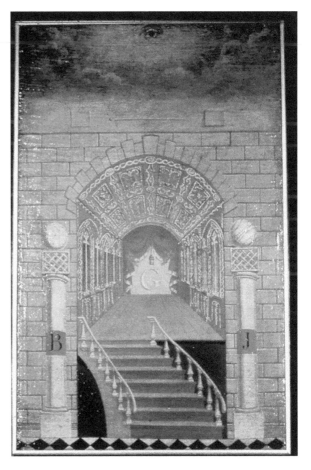

Q. On what ground do our Lodges stand?

A. Holy ground.

Q. Why on holy ground?

A. Because the first lodge was consecrated.

The mention of holy ground in a Masonic context takes as its reference Chapter 3 of the Book of Exodus, in which Moses has an encounter with an angel on Mount Horeb:

> *And the angel of the Lord appeared unto him in a flame of fire out of the midst of a bush: and he looked, and, behold, the bush burned with fire, and the bush was not consumed. And Moses said, I will now turn aside, and see this great sight, why the bush was not burnt. And … God called out to him out of the midst of the bush … and he said, Draw not nigh hither: put off thy shoes from off thy feet, for the place whereon thou standest is holy ground.*

There is a very individual depiction of the square pavement. On the second degree board, the pillars are in the opposite arrangement to present-day practice, and the all-seeing eye appears again. A more conventional form of the square pavement appears at the bottom. The third degree board shows a number of features associated with other degrees, notably the ladder, the Bible, the point-within-a-circle-between-two-grand-parallel-lines, the three steps, the orders of architecture, unusual for a third degree board, and the numerals 3-5-7-9-11-15, for which there is no definitive explanation. The numbers 3-5-7 are clear enough, and it has been suggested that 11 refers to one exchange in the exposure *Three Distinct Knocks* of 1760:

Q. Why should Eleven make a Lodge, Brother?

A. There were Eleven Patriarchs, when Joseph was sold into Egypt, and suppos'd to be lost.

The number 15 may, of course, refer to the three Lodges each of five Fellow Crafts. But the number 9 could have a number of connotations, one being the nine muses. This is one of the few third degree boards which shows the figure of Hiram Abiff in graphic detail. This board appears to have been painted in 1815.

In 1779 the Pilgrim Lodge, today No. 238, was founded in London under the Modern Grand Lodge. The founders counted among their number several courtiers at the Court of King George III and since the Court was largely German speaking at that time, a number of German-speaking Freemasons were keen to found a Lodge working the ritual in German. The Lodge worked, in the first instance, according to the Swedish Zinnendorf ritual, but changed then to the Schröder ritual in the 19th century. Its ritual, copying the practice of the times in Germany and other countries, made use not of tracing boards as such, but of a carpet, into which the symbols had been woven.

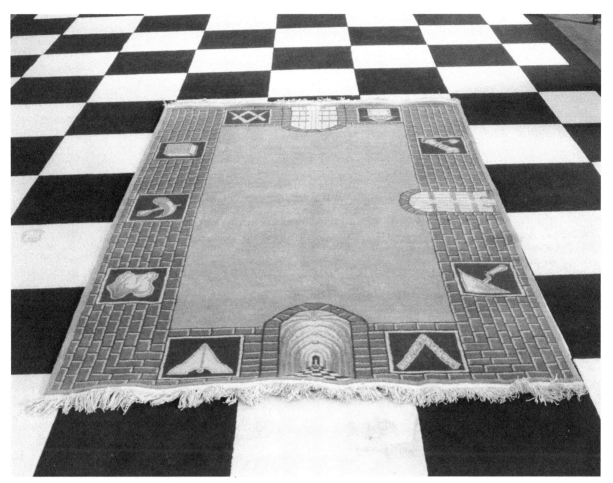

Above: Lodge carpet of the Pilgrim Lodge

Overleaf: Lodge carpet laid out with three Lesser Lights

The symbols woven into it are, clockwise from top left, the square and compasses, the east entrance to the Temple, a beehive, a plumb line, the south entrance, a trowel, a square, the west entrance to the temple, a level, a rough ashlar, a *Spitzhammer* or pickhammer, and a Bible. The west entrance to the temple is said in that ritual to be the route by which Hiram's body was dragged out of the temple. The *Spitzhammer* or pickhammer is the working tool with which the Apprentice works on the rough ashlar to make it perfect, as opposed to the gavel and chisel used in English-speaking Lodges. This lodge carpet has a central role in the ceremonial. At the opening of the Lodge it is laid out ceremonially by the Deacons, the Ionic, Doric and Corinthian pillars are placed in position, and the candles are ceremonially lit by the Deacon.

The carpet is a near-sacred space. Only candidates for initiation and Grand Masters are permitted to walk over it. This carpet and the ceremonial attached to it mirror very closely the practice in many German and other continental Lodges.

In a sense, therefore, this carpet marks a transition point, from our consideration of symbolism in the Lodges of the United Grand Lodge of England, to that of Lodges in other countries and other jurisdictions, which forms the basis for our next and final chapter.

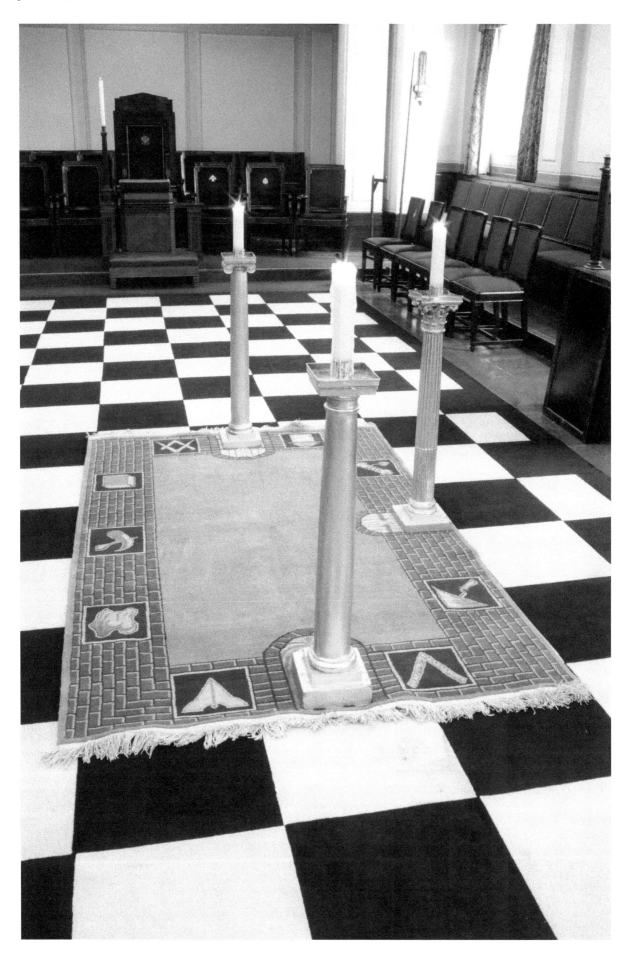

TRACING BOARDS BEYOND THE UNITED GRAND LODGE OF ENGLAND

Below left: Frontispiece of Mahhabone

Below right: The 'Véritable Plan' for a Lodge of Apprentices (first degree) and Companions (second degree) in France from 1745

Although tracing boards are probably as widely used in Lodges of the United Grand Lodge of England as in any other country in the world, nonetheless floor cloths, carpets and the many variants of this Masonic artefact have been in use in other jurisdictions throughout the world from earliest times. We are not going to attempt a comprehensive review in all countries and in all centuries, but we hope to review many different strands to show their relationship to, and divergence from, each other.

Less than 100 km across the English Channel, closer to London than, say, Oxford, are many early records of lodge cloths. Some of the earliest Masonic exposures came from France, and even the frontispiece to *Mahhabone* that we looked at in Chapter 4 shows evidence of French influence.

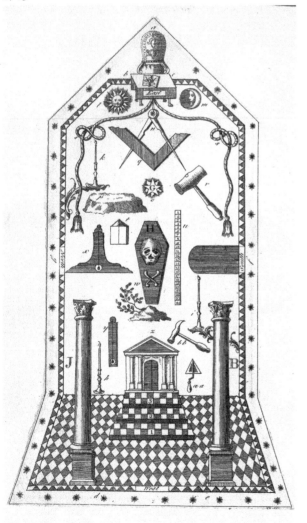
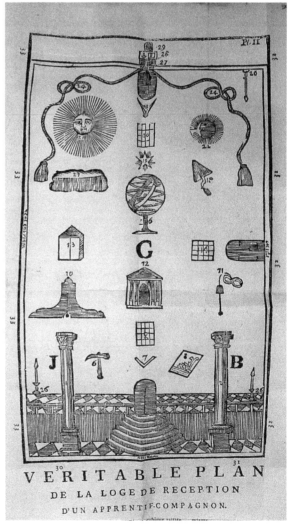

Among the points these two illustrations have in common are:

- the three 'lights' in the form of candles, east, south and west

- the pointed cubic stone, an emblem otherwise unknown in English Freemasonry

- the trowel

- the cord with tassels

- the diamond-form mosaic pavement

- the pickhammer.

All of these indicate a continental European influence. Note also, in the *Véritable Plan* on the right, the Armillary Sphere, just under the blazing star.

The *Véritable Plan* on page 65 is the precursor of the two French boards shown below, on the left that of the Apprentice, on the right that of Companion or Fellow Craft. These two date from the year 1821. Note the differences between them. In the first board, we have three steps, in the second, seven. The second board features a blazing star, a letter G, a diamond-form mosaic pavement, and a crossed ruler and crowbar. Like the *Véritable Plan* on the previous page, there are three windows with grilles, east, south and west. The positions of the pillars Boaz and Jachin have been reversed, the trowel has disappeared, and a rigid plumb rule has taken the place of the plumb line. The Armillary Sphere has disappeared, and stars have been inserted.

18th century French first and second degree tracing boards from Delaulnay's Thuileur

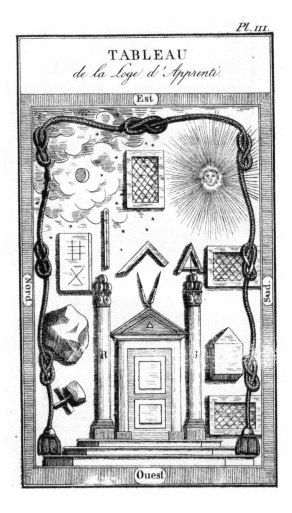

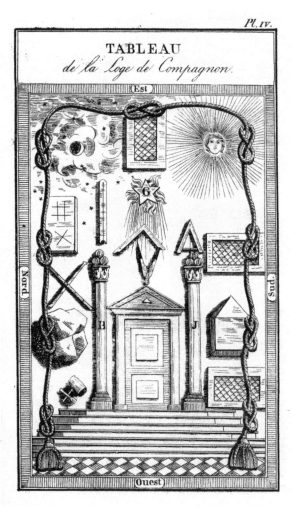

A very striking feature is the *Houpe Dentelée* or so-called indented tuft, a cord twining round the board's edge with a tassel at each end. This is a common theme to many continental European boards and is a symbol of strength and union, the cord with knots being also indicative of a measuring device. In some Lodges themselves the cord, starting at the Senior Warden's column in the north west – both Wardens being in the west in many continental Lodges – passes round the temple at mid-height, through the north, east and south, ending at the other column, symbolising a protective enclosure. In this symbolic sense, it fulfils the purpose of the indented border in English tracing boards. Note also the inverted arrangement of the square, angle upwards, and compasses, angle downwards.

The three windows seem to be specific to French boards. One justification for them seems clear from Prichard's expose:

Q. Have you any fix'd Lights in your Lodge?

A. Yes.

Q. How many?

A. Three.

Q. How are they situated?

A. East, South and West.

Q. What are their Uses?

A. To light the Men to, at and from their Work.

Q. Why are there no Lights in the North?

A. Because the Sun darts no Rays from thence.

The pointed cubic stone is of particular interest. On French boards, the simple perfect six-sided ashlar, as featured on English boards, is unknown. In its place is the pointed cubic stone, that is a properly dressed cube surmounted by a four-sided pyramid. Irène Mainguy in *La Symbolique Maçonnique du Troisième Millénaire* has this to say:

> *The four lateral faces of the cube are a reminder of the four cardinal points, while the pyramidion underlines the importance of the zenith … The centre of the square of the base fixes the sacred point …and the vertical axis, rising towards the point of the pyramid, indicates the direction of ascent to the summit of the mountain, towards which the initiate should strive, and which can be understood as access to pure spirituality.*

Compare the two boards on page 66 with the present-day design of a combined first and second degree board shown overleaf. Here we have the indented border of the English boards, the seven stars, the far shorter tufted cord, and the seven steps, which, far from commencing *on* the mosaic pavement, give access to it.

There is the odd addition of an axe above the pointed cubic stone. This may be the representation of a broach or masonic axe. However, some French scholars adhere to the theory that, in early representations of these symbols, this emblem was in fact a square, which became corrupted by repeated copying into the shape of an axe.

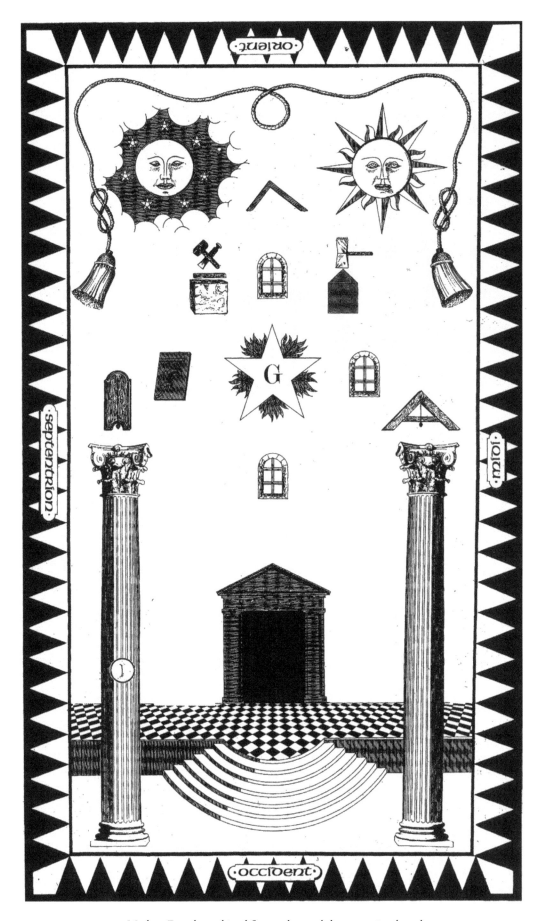

Modern French combined first and second degree tracing board

Interestingly the cardinal point of north is represented by the word *septentrion*, having an allusion to the seven stars of the Great Bear constellation, and therefore indicating also the north, a double inference for Freemasons. The position of south is likewise referred to as *midi*, midday, the hour of high noon.

The board on page 68 is doubtless the offspring of the board shown here, from the 18th century in France, where the temple is an altogether more splendid structure, the pillars far more imposing, the perspective better defined. The Latin inscription *'Fidelitas moribus unita'* has so far defied an adequate translation. The Boaz pillar is named *Sagesse* (wisdom), the Jachin pillar *Force* (strength) but *Beauté* (beauty) is reserved for the east end of the board, near the blazing star, a slightly different arrangement to modern-day English practice.

The old French representation of the third degree on page 70, dating from the year 1821 does not present English Freemasons with many enigmas. The one characteristic feature which is repeated many times in this degree is the depiction of tear drops. Note the diamond-form mosaic pavement.

In the present-day third degree board on page 71, the tear-drop motif is used much more liberally, but the whole board presents a much more sober, austere aspect: the indented border, four entrances to the temple, a simple outline of a coffin, the square and compasses not united, and seven steps as in the second degree board above.

Note the present-day layout of a French temple of the Grande Loge de France on page 72. The three Lesser Lights are situated at the corners of the floor cloth itself, in an arrangement reminiscent of that of the Pilgrim Lodge shown at the end of Chapter 4. The square pavement is just visible under the floor cloth. Note the rough ashlar at the left, counter-balanced by the pointed cubic stone to the right, one step up.

Travelling south east from Paris, across the Jura mountains, over the border and then through Switzerland and Austria, almost to the border with Slovakia, we come to Vienna, the home of one of the oldest lodge cloths in existence (shown on page 73). This cloth, 2.10 m x 0.92 m (*c*.82.5 in. x 36 in.), was found in 1860 during works carried out to extend the city of Vienna. It was buried in an iron box, and may have been hidden there when the Vienna Lodges were suspended in 1794. It is painted on leather, not mounted, and its condition,

18th century French combined first and second degree tracing board

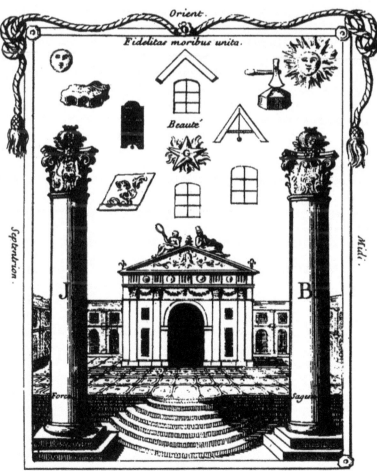

69

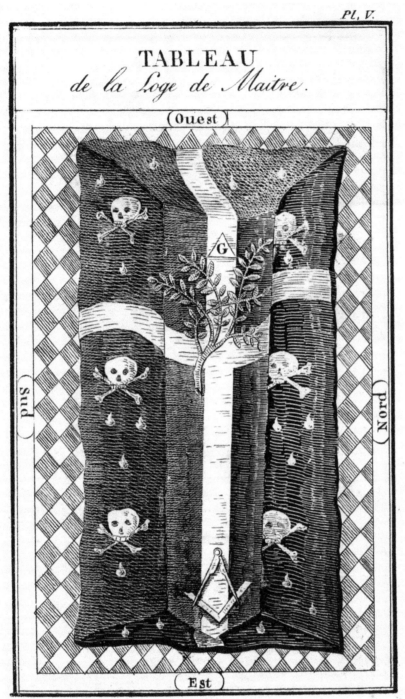

18th century French third degree tracing board from Delaulnay's Thuileur

after so many years and in view of the manner in which it was buried, is little short of amazing. It has been dated to 1780, and the museum catalogue states that it is a second degree 'carpet' or floor cloth. We see the cord of union with its tassels, as on the French boards, the 'gallows' square, the sun and moon, the blazing star with the letter G, rough and perfect ashlars, plumb rule, tracing board, level, trowel, compasses, gavel and stairway with seven steps, but in common with the French boards we have looked at, there is no Bible. The two pillars are surmounted by globes on which signs of the zodiac are depicted, rather than the celestial and terrestrial globes. The pillar on the left as viewed in the illustration is identified by the letter 'I'. This marks it as the Jachin pillar, Iachin being an alternative spelling. The indented border is well defined, as is the pyramid-form mosaic pavement.

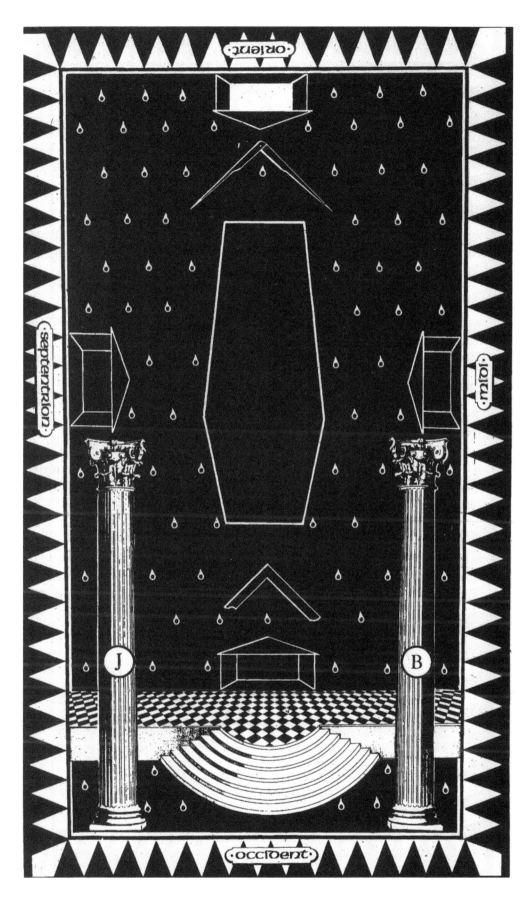

French third degree tracing board

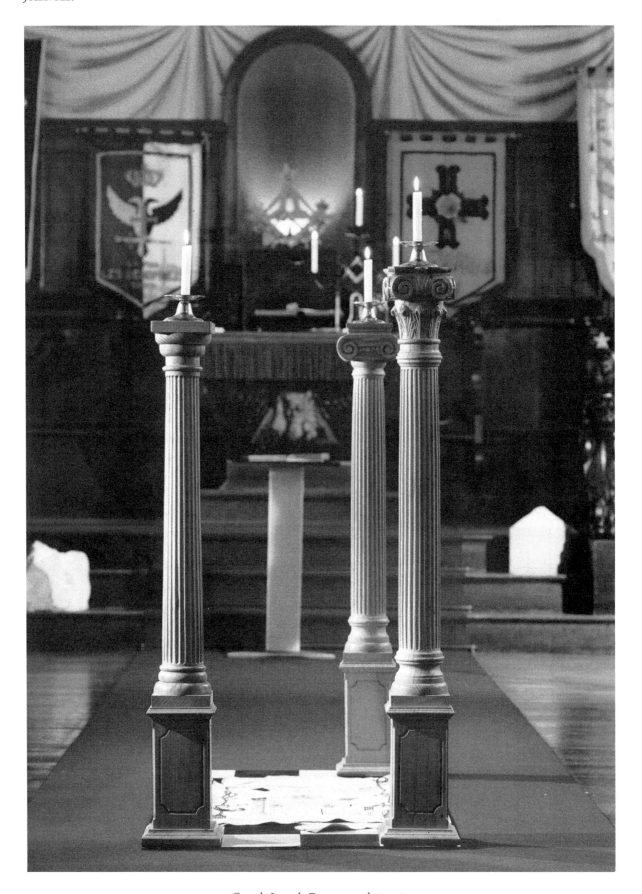

Grande Loge de France temple interior

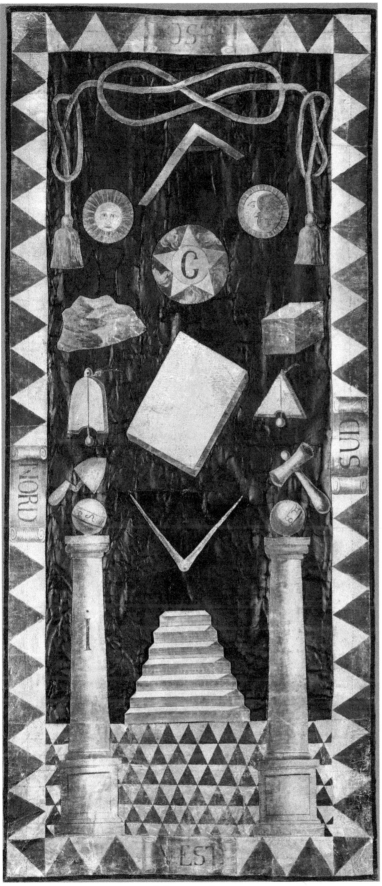

Austrian lodge carpet c. 1780

This very old lodge cloth has served as the model for a reconstruction, which is in use today, shown overleaf in the Museum of Freemasonry at Rosenau Castle in Austria.

On page 75 are two examples of modern boards designed for a Lodge in Linz, in Austria, and show an austere, uncluttered approach. On the first board on the left we see the cord of union, moon, sun, rough ashlar, pickhammer, perfect ashlar, square and compasses, twenty-four-inch gauge, Bible open at St. John's Gospel *'Im Anfong war das Wort'* (In the beginning was the Word), pillars, of which only one is labelled, plumb rule, square pavement with three rows and symbols specific to the Lodge to which the board belongs. The second board features a much longer cord, without knots, the blazing star and letter G, crossed chisels – one pointed, one flat – gavel, trowel, three ears of corn, level, and between the pillars the Bible, square and compasses. We see pomegranates atop the pillars, both of which are labelled, seven steps, entrances east, south and west and square pavement with five rows.

A third degree board (shown on page 76), belonging to the Mozart Lodge in Vienna, carries on the tear-drop motif we saw in the French boards. In a striking change in symbolism the four points of the compass are marked 'Auffgang', 'Mittag', 'Nidergang' and 'Mitnacht', namely sunrise, midday, sunset and midnight. The tetragrammaton, acacia, skull and cross bones decorate the coffin, and the ritual progression of steps is marked out. As a general rule, continental European boards in the third degree have a tendency to be much more sober than in England, reminding us of the bleak message at the beginning of this supreme degree.

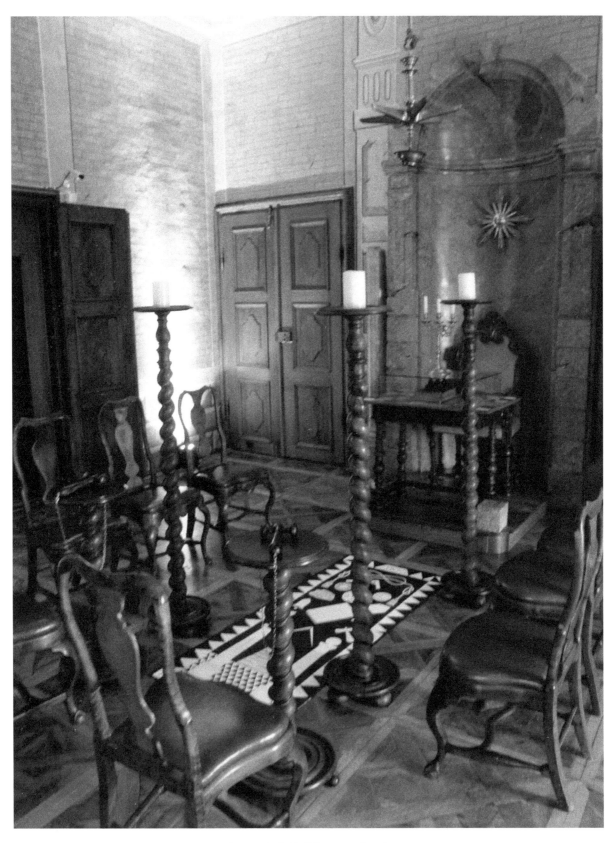

A room in Schloß Rosenau, Austria

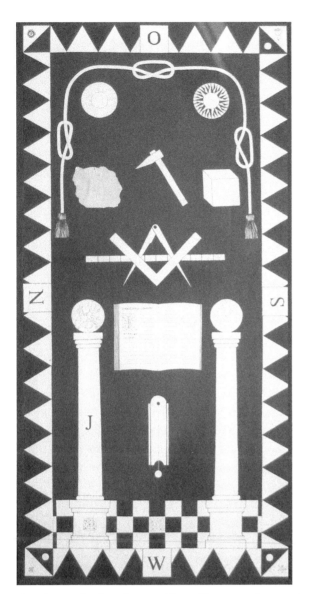

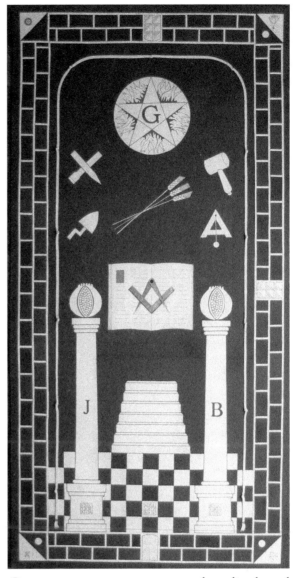

Austrian tracing boards first and second degrees, 20th century

Travelling north now into Germany we come across a much earlier board (shown overleaf), said to date from *c.*1760, and said to have been used originally in France. Unusually for a French board it is coloured. We see here the knotted cord, the three windows, sun and moon, triangle containing the tetragrammaton or name of God, rendered as the four Hebrew letters yod-he-vau-he, or יהוה. We see the blazing star with the symbol Γ in red – the Greek letter Gamma standing for Geometry, but which is also the image of a 'gallows' square – the tracing board, plumb rule, level, the square and compasses inverted, the pillars labelled the opposite way to accepted English practice, crossed chisels – one pointed, one flat – a rough ashlar, pointed cubic stone, gavel and pickhammer and diamond-form pavement. The 'gallows' square, in which one arm is longer than the other, is a feature of many lodge boards and carpets in continental Europe.

On page 77 is an old board, with marked French influence, designed for the first and second degrees. The windows have been inserted above the doorways in the east, south and west. This board dates from the mid-19th century, and surmounting the Iachin pillar is a gyroscope or primitive astrolabe while a simple terrestrial globe adorns the other. There is a paucity of jewels or working tools. Either side of the doorway in the east are the plumb line and level and the pillars are flanked by the two ashlars.

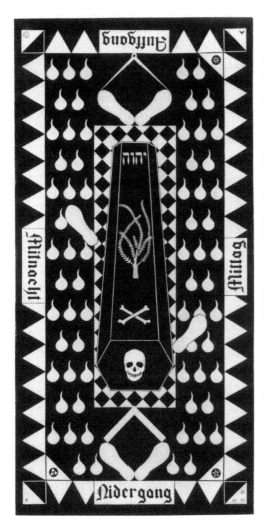
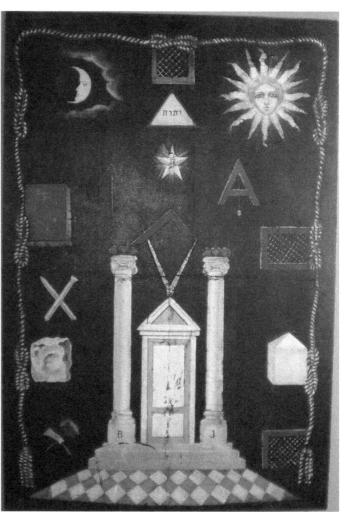

Above left: Austrian third degree tracing board, 20th century

Above right: French tracing board c. 1760

The board at the top of page 78 was designed to include symbolism of the first and second degrees, a feature characteristic of northern European boards. The moon is surrounded by eight stars, the five-pointed star by five tongues of flame. Two pickhammers are employed, one on each ashlar, and the tracing board itself is supported on an easel and rests on the twenty-four-inch gauge. The symbolism is completed by gavel, trowel, plumb line, level and square and compasses. The depiction of King Solomon's Temple is that of Palladian architecture, another feature often found in German boards.

At the foot of page 78 is another example of a woven carpet, belonging to a Lodge of the Grand Lodge Zu den Drei Weltkugeln (Three Globes). The blazing star is six-pointed and occupies the top centre of the carpet. Apart from the usual emblems at the top of the boards we see nine stars, referring to the nine muses. The Temple is of a modified Palladian style, and the all-seeing eye is clearly visible on the pediment. Gavel, pickhammer, chisel and square are arranged round a piece of stonework at lower right, on a level with the two ashlars. The most striking features of this carpet however are the three doorways, which, unlike most boards and carpets, appear to be placed south, west and north.

On page 79 is a carpet of a modern design for the Grand Lodge Zu den Drei Weltkugeln. In Germany and Austria, more than anywhere else, the design of tracing boards and carpets has been subject to a new and invigorating impetus in the second half of the 20th century, and this board shows the

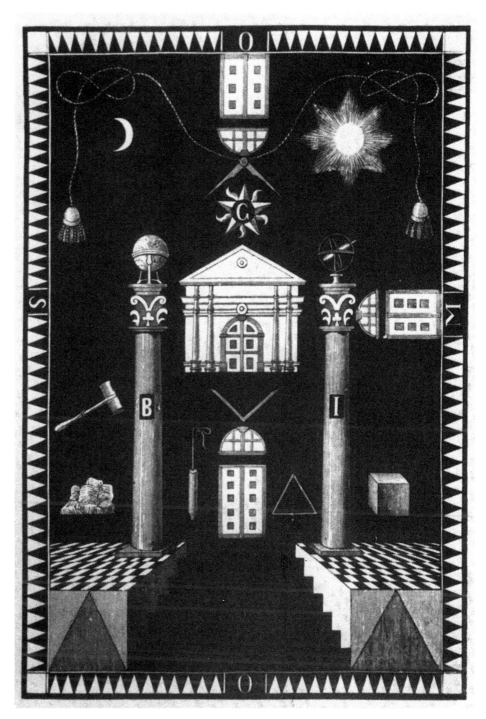

German tracing board, mid-19th century

resurgence of artistic endeavour in recent years. When we consider that many Masonic artefacts were destroyed under fascism and communism from 1933 until the fall of the Iron Curtain, it is quite natural that there should now be a blossoming of artistic endeavour, and today many Lodges in central and Eastern Europe are producing new, bold and interesting designs as a result. We might almost regard this as a sort of Masonic renaissance.

If we travel further north, we enter the realms of the Nordic Rite, which is practised by Lodges in all Scandinavian countries. On page 80 are boards of 18th century design, on the left the first degree, the second degree in the middle and the third degree on the right. There are a few significant differences between the first and second boards. The first board shows pyramid-form pavement, and only one pillar, Jachin, labelled. The second board shows seven steps and an empty tracing board. Interestingly, although the Nordic Rite ritual is said to have come from England via France, the perfect ashlar is shown as it is recognised in England, namely six-sided, and not the pointed cubic stone we met with when examining French boards. The third degree board is quite reminiscent of the French style.

On page 81 is a modern-day Nordic Rite first and second degree tracing board. We first of all notice striking resemblances to both French and German boards. Moon, inverted square and sun make the first row of very neatly ordered symbols, then the two ashlars and the blazing star with the letter G, trowel to the left and gavel to the right, plumb line, tracing board and level and last, between the pillars, the inverted compasses. The pillars stand *on* the square pavement, reminiscent of *Mahhabone* and reflecting the German and Austrian practice, in contrast to the French boards and cloths which more often show the pillars *in front of* the square pavement. The seven steps lead *up to* the square pavement, as in many French boards, unlike the German boards where the steps start *on* the square pavement. Nowadays the Nordic Rite makes use only of boards in the first and second degrees – in the third degree, the symbols are concrete, three-dimensional objects, having no need of depiction in this two-dimensional way.

As can be imagined, there is an infinite variety of tracing boards in all countries of continental Europe, and there are many that we have not covered here. Moreover, if we cross the Atlantic, we encounter a richer spectrum, stemming from the particular New World cultures which, although

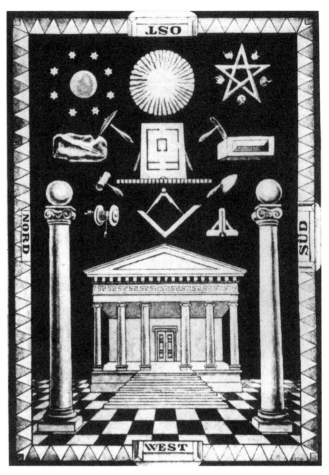

Above: German tracing board mid-19th century

Below: Lodge carpet for the Großloge Zu den Drei Weltkugeln c. 1960

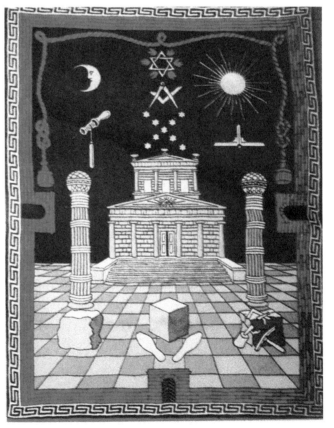

influenced by European origins, have overlaid the symbolism with uniquely North American artistic and cultural influences. We should note, at the outset, that lodge cloths and tracing boards do not feature in present-day ritual in the USA. Brent Morris, Editor of *The Scottish Rite Journal of Freemasonry, Southern Jurisdiction* and author of several Masonic publications in the USA, tells us that

> *Except for a handful of lodges that work Emulation or other English rituals, tracing boards are merely historical curiosities. The individual pieces from the tracing board plus other images illustrating the lectures were extracted and made into slides. This started in the 1800s with oil-burning magic lanterns and hand-painted glass slides.*

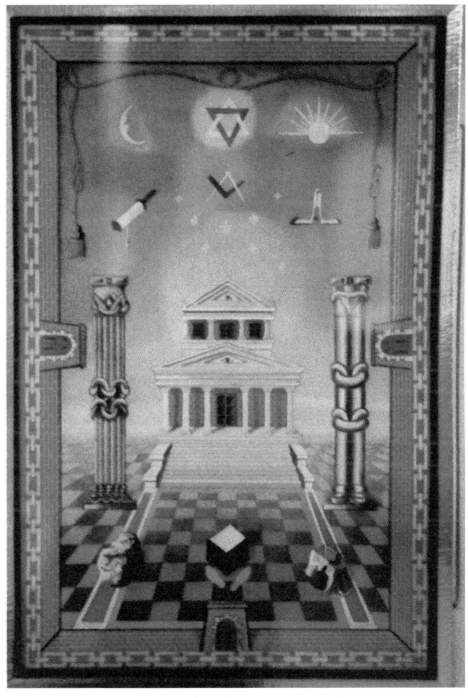

Lodge carpet for the Großloge Zu den Drei Weltkugeln

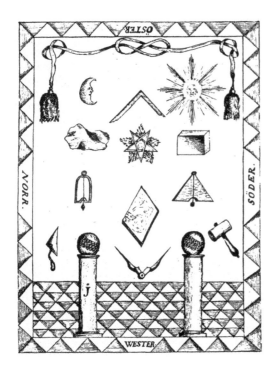
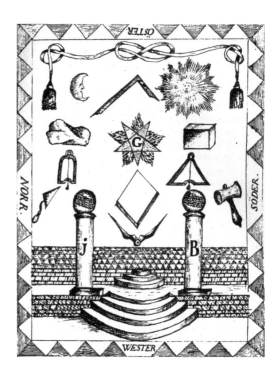

The old boards and cloths have however been preserved as historical artefacts.

For a good illustration of how old-world origins have been transplanted, we have only to view the two illustrations on page 82. The illustration on the left is from the frontispiece of *The Builder's Jewel* by Thomas and Batty Langley, London 1741, and that on the right is from a tracing board, artist unknown, from St. Andrew's Lodge, No. 289, of Hobart, New York, *c.*1800, oil on canvas. It was almost certainly a lodge cloth before being mounted and framed. The artist has replaced the landscape with a square pavement, three steps, and a fragment of an indented border. He has also copied Langley's incongruous order of the pillars as Doric (wisdom), Ionic (strength) and Corinthian (beauty). Langley already has the three Great Lights on the left-hand pillar, the three movable jewels on the right, a tracing board on the centre pillar together with a clock and the Latin numerals III, V and VII on the pillar bases. In addition, he has on the centre pillar, a depiction of the wind of Freemasonry we mentioned earlier, which blows 'favourably, due east or west'. Langley added two other letters which we know to mean H(oly) G(round). The artist of the board on the right appears to have overlooked this, but has added seven stars, a ladder with figures ascending, a blazing star, sword, key and winged hourglass. The *Freemason's Monitor or Illustrations of Masonry* by Thomas Smith Webb, published towards the end of the 19th century in the USA, regarding the little particles in the winged hourglass, tells us:

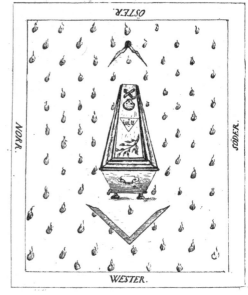

Three Nordic Rite tracing boards 18th century

> *… in the short space of an hour, they are all exhausted. Thus wastes man! today he puts forth the tender leaves of hope; tomorrow, blossoms and bears his blushing honors thick upon him; the next day comes a frost, which nips the shoot, and when he thinks his greatness is still aspiring, he falls, like autumn leaves, to enrich our mother earth.*

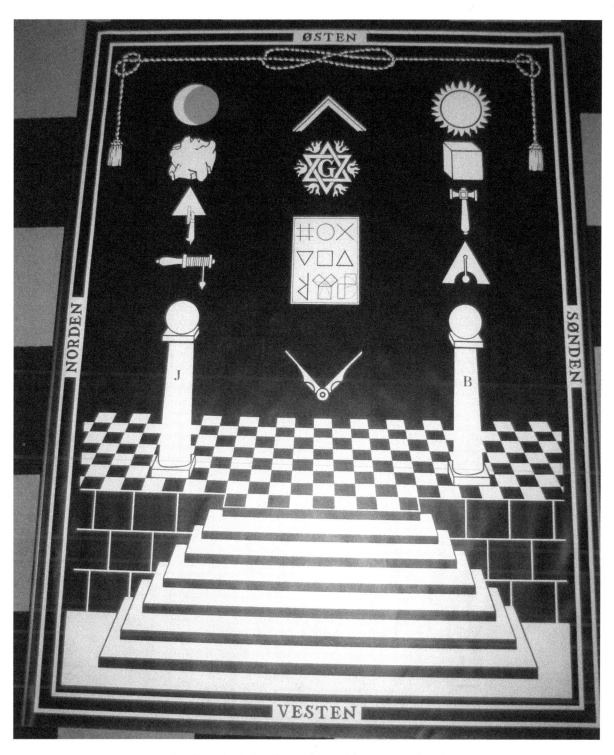

Modern Nordic Rite first and second degree tracing board

The artist has also added a pot of incense, which, according to *The True Masonic Chart, or Hieroglyphic Monitor* of 1819 by Jeremy Cross, is

> *... an emblem of a pure heart, which is always an acceptable sacrifice to the Deity; and, as this glows with fervent heat, so should our hearts continually glow with gratitude to the great beneficent Author of our existence, for the manifold blessings and comforts we enjoy.*

The artist has also added a gavel, trowel and twenty-four-inch gauge. The bust atop the Corinthian pillar on both illustrations, being labelled 'MM', we may assume to refer to Hiram Abiff and all Master Masons since.

Around 1800, says the American authority Professor William Moore, these ritual paintings began to be exhibited vertically within a lodge room rather than laid flat on the floor. On the opposite page and on page 84 we have two lodge cloths with more than a passing similarity to their English forebears.

The cloth on the opposite page is painted in oils on fabric and may even have been made in England and exported to the colony of Carolina. It belongs to Royal White Hart Lodge No. 2 in Halifax, North Carolina, and is dated at between 1764 and 1772. All the usual first degree symbolism is contained in this board, with some important additions and variations. There is a pot of incense and a winged hourglass as well as a twenty-four-inch gauge, and in addition to the more conventional plumb rule we see a hand appearing from the clouds, supporting a plumb line. This relates to a portion of scripture applied here in the second degree, the Book of Amos, chap. vii, verses 7-8:

Left: Frontispiece to The Builder's Jewel, London, 1741

Right: Tracing board, New York, c.1800

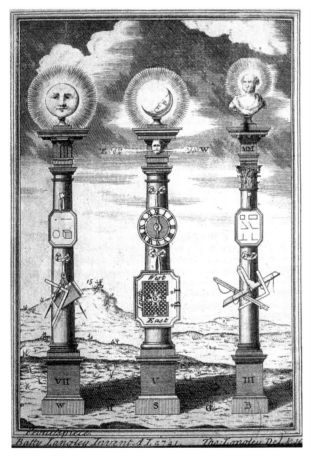

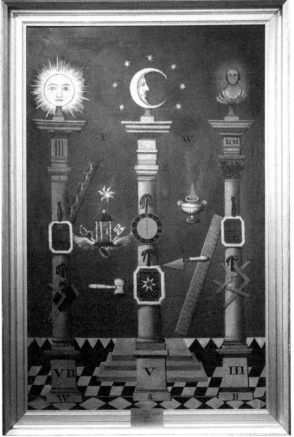

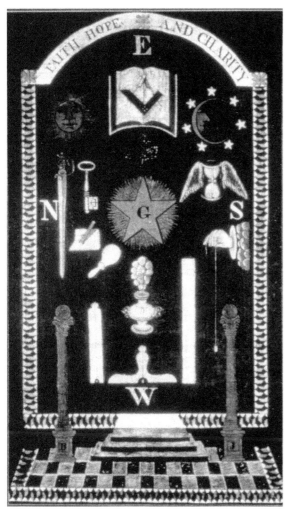

Lodge cloth, North Carolina, c.1770

Thus he shewed me and, behold, the Lord stood upon a wall made by a plumbline, with a plumbline in his hand. And the Lord said unto me, Amos, what seest thou? And I said, A plumbline. Then said the Lord, Behold, I will set a plumbline in the midst of my people Israel: I will not again pass by them any more.

There is no separate square as a movable jewel, and the tesselated border is of an individualistic design.

The more stylised board on page 84 combines symbolism of the first and second degrees. On the pediment below the pot of incense flanked by two cherubs are the words *Sit Lux et Lux Fuit* (Let there be light, and there was light). To the left is a sword lying across the Book of Constitutions. The *Freemason's Monitor or Illustrations of Masonry* says that

The Book of Constitutions, guarded by the Tiler's sword, reminds us that we should ever be watchful and guarded in our thoughts, words and actions, particularly when before the enemies of Masonry; ever bearing in remembrance those truly Masonic virtues, silence and circumspection.

We also see an hourglass and the 47th proposition from the first book of Euclid. A sword pointing at a heart is a common symbol in American Freemasonry, and

… demonstrates that justice will sooner or later overtake us; and although our thoughts, words and actions may be hidden from the eyes of man, yet that All-Seeing Eye, whom the sun, moon and stars obey, and under whose watchful care even comets perform their stupendous revolutions, pervades the inmost recesses of the human heart, and will reward us according to our merits.

Below this we see depictions of the five orders of architecture and a motif which appears to be a tent next to a half-finished building. In the centre of the pavement is a seven-pointed star, and beyond it the winding staircase leading to the middle chamber beneath the letter G suspended from the archway. To the right we see the trowel and a beehive. In the words of *The True Masonic Chart* the beehive

… is an emblem of industry, and recommends the practice of that virtue to all created beings, from the highest seraph in heaven to the lowest reptile of the dust. It teaches us that, as we came into the world rational and intelligent beings, so we should ever be industrious ones, never sitting down contented while our fellow-creatures around us are in want, when it is in our power to relieve them without inconvenience to ourselves.

Beneath this is an anchor and Noah's ark which, according to *The True Masonic Chart*

> *... are emblems of a well-grounded hope and a well-spent life. They are emblematical of that divine Ark which safely wafts us over this tempestuous sea of troubles, and that Anchor which shall safely moor us in a peaceful harbor, where the wicked cease from troubling and the weary shall find rest.*

Beneath these are the three movable jewels. Lower down are the three Lesser Lights surrounding the three Great Lights and a small Jacob's Ladder with the initials of (F)aith, (H)ope and (C)harity. At the foot of the board we see the rough ashlar, a pickhammer, the twenty-four-inch gauge, perfect ashlar, charcoal, chalk and clay, the point-within-a-circle between-two-grand-parallel-lines supporting the Bible, and the third immovable jewel, the tracing board itself. The whole is surmounted by the sun, moon, seven stars and all-seeing eye.

Below: Tracing board by Jonas Prentiss, 1818

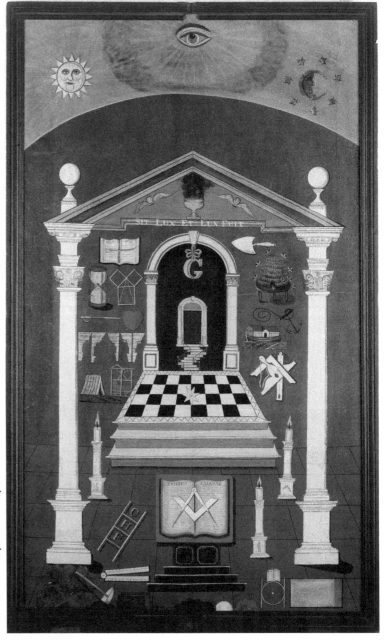

The lodge cloth on the opposite page, by contrast, displays symbolism from all three Craft degrees, and some from the Holy Royal Arch degree. It is from the Widow's Son Lodge, No. 60, of Milton, Virginia, and shows evidence of an earlier painting under the present one. We notice the lack of the four cardinal points of the compass. There is a prominent arch and keystone and above the keystone appears to be a Book of Constitutions. Other symbols are, from the top right-hand side clockwise, the sun, gavel, crossed quills, ladder, flaming sword, level, plumb rule, key, sword, coffin, square, anchor, trowel, compasses and twenty-four-inch gauge, triangle with letter G, Noah's ark and dove, moon and seven stars. In the centre between the pillars we see the glory and all-seeing eye, three Lesser Lights, three Great Lights and the square pavement once again at the top of the three steps rather than beneath them.

The illustration on page 86 is of an engraving by Thomas Kensett, published in Connecticut in 1812, entitled 'Master's Carpet Compleat', printed on paper, *c.*40 cm x 33 cm (16 in. x l3in.). This was apparently used both as a print in its own right and as an ornamentation on aprons. In this design we can see the American artistic genius moving away significantly from the European templates which influenced much early work. Strikingly the illustration is in the form of a building, an allegory perhaps of the 'ethereal mansion, not made with hands, eternal in the heavens'. It has been designed on four levels, of which the top three correspond to the three Craft degrees. The whole is supported by the Ionic, Doric and Corinthian pillars and three tools, twenty-four-inch gauge, common gavel and pickhammer, to be used on the rough ashlar. Above that, we have the three Great Lights, three Lesser Lights and altar on the mosaic pavement between two colonnades each of seven pillars, denoting the seven who make a perfect Lodge. On this level also are the sword, perfect ashlar and cable-tow. On the next level we see the square, level and plumb rule and the letter G between two colonnades each of five pillars, denoting the five who hold a Lodge. The level after that shows two colonnades each of three pillars, since three rule a Lodge. It also displays the anchor, hourglass, coffin and scythe, which according to the *Freemason's Monitor or Illustrations of Masonry* is an emblem of time:

> *... if, by chance, we should escape the numerous evils incident to childhood and youth, and with health and vigor arrive to the years of manhood; yet, withal, we must soon be cut down by the all-devouring scythe of Time, and be gathered into the land where our fathers have gone before us.*

Below: Lodge cloth, Charlottesville, Virginia, c.1800

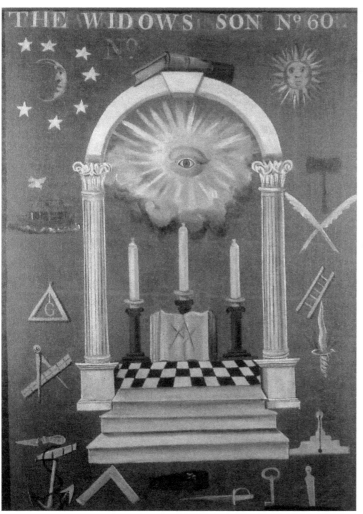

Next to the scythe are a shovel, sprig of acacia, heavy maul, five-pointed star, trowel, altar and the egress from the temple to the countryside, where Hiram Abiff's body was found buried. Above the two swags are the words 'Hail! heavenly Virtue! thine's a Sacred flame' beneath the figure of Charity. At her feet, to the left, we can just make out what appear to be the three ruffians hiding in the cavern, reminiscent of the Josiah Bowring board on page 57. Above and to the right we see a comet, to the left a sword pointing at a heart, counterbalanced on the right by a sword and Book of Constitutions. At far left is the Bible resting on the circle-between-two-parallel-lines motif, balanced on the far right by Jacob's Ladder linking earth and heaven. Crowning the whole image is the all-seeing eye in the centre of an immense glory above the clouds. The three emblems next to the left-hand pillar are the scales of justice, the beehive, and Noah's ark and a dove. These are

85

balanced on the right by clasped hands, a pot of incense and Euclid's 47th proposition. The two pillars flanking the whole are two of the most splendid we have encountered on any tracing board, with their very ornate celestial and terrestrial globes.

The influence of this engraving has undoubtedly given rise to many cloths and boards, two of which are shown on page 87 and page 88.

Master's Carpet Compleat by Thomas Kensett, 1812

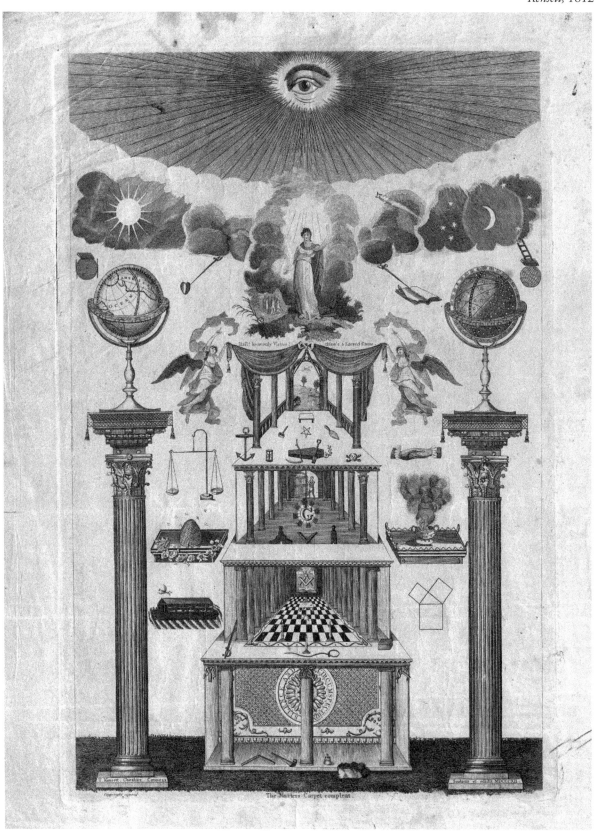

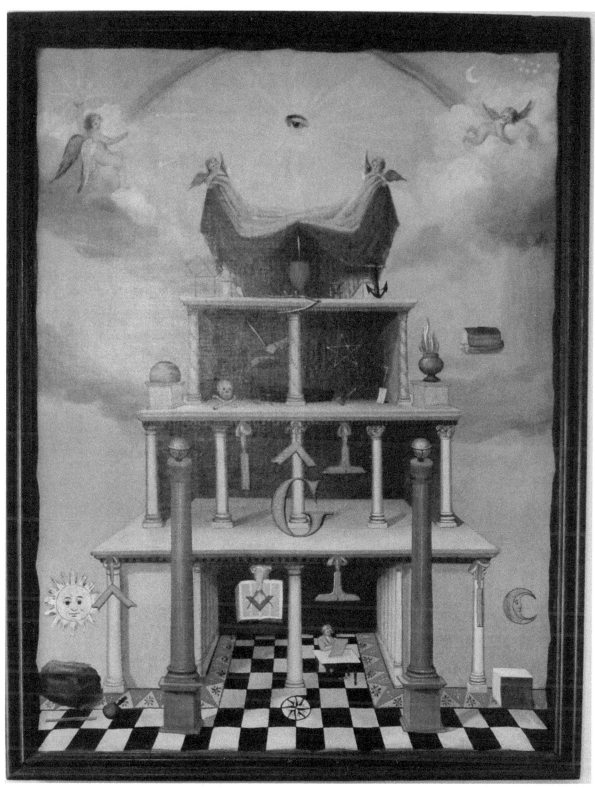

Tracing board, Western Star Lodge, Bridgewater, New York

This is a lodge cloth, artist unknown, oil on canvas, *c.*1810. It was owned by the Western Star Lodge, No. 15, in Bridgewater in New York State. The two main pillars are far less prominent. Note that a rather intricate coloured tesselated boder has been introduced, the figure guarding the door on the second degree level has been removed, but the Master, sitting at his tracing board on the first level, as a counterpoint to the hand of the Almighty handing down the Bible, square and compasses, has been reproduced from the 'Master's Carpet Cornpleat'. This is reminiscent of the fifth section of the first Emulation lecture:

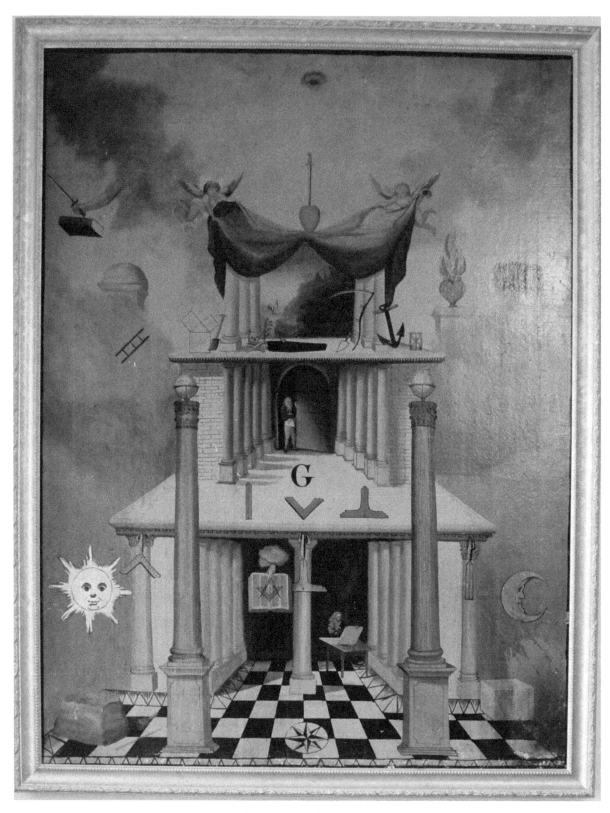

Tracing board, Cherry Valley Lodge, Cherry Valley, New York

As the tracing board is for the Master to lay lines and draw designs on, the better to enable the Brethren to carry on the intended structure with regularity and propriety, so the Volume of the Sacred Law may justly be deemed the spiritual tracing board of the Great Architect of the Universe, in which are laid down such divine laws and moral plans, that were we conversant therein and adherent thereto, would bring us to an ethereal mansion, not made with hands, eternal in the heavens.

Three tracing boards of the International Order of Freemasonry Le Droit Humain

On the opposite page is a lodge cloth, also oil on canvas, from the Cherry Valley Lodge, No. 334 in New York State, probably by the same artist. In this illustration, the four storeys have been reduced to three, but the colonnade arrangement of seven, five and three which we saw in the 'Master's Carpet Compleat' has been reproduced. The figure guarding the door in the second degree has been re-introduced. All the other symbols are present on this cloth.

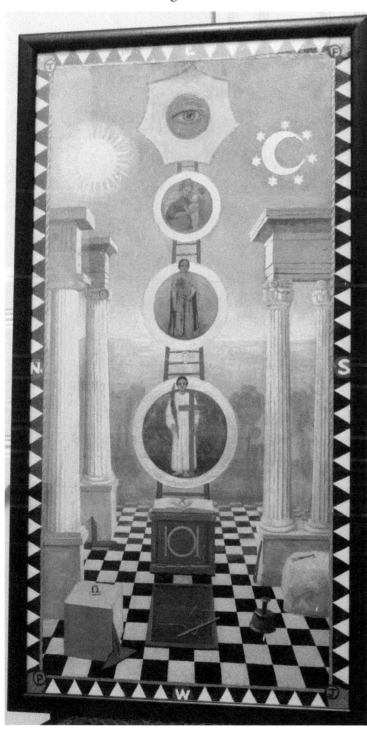

Our journey has been a long one in distance, but not so copious in the number of boards we have had the space to explore. There are however three more boards in England which amply repay a little study. These are the boards of the International Order of Freemasonry Le Droit Humain.

The first degree board on the left is distinguished by very prominent figures of Faith, Hope and Charity, with the addition, at the top of the ladder, of a seven-pointed blazing star or glory and an all-seeing eye. The cardinal virtues are distinguished, apart from their tassels, by their initial letters. The second degree board (overleaf) has very striking Egyptian influence in its design but, in addition to the ear of corn and fall of water in the lower section, there is a most interesting feature by the side of the staircase, namely a perfect, or perfected, ashlar, with a gavel and chisel lying on it, a symbol that the Fellow Craft has achieved his work. The third degree board on the right shows all the emblems we are used to from the John Harris board, but viewed from inside the grave.

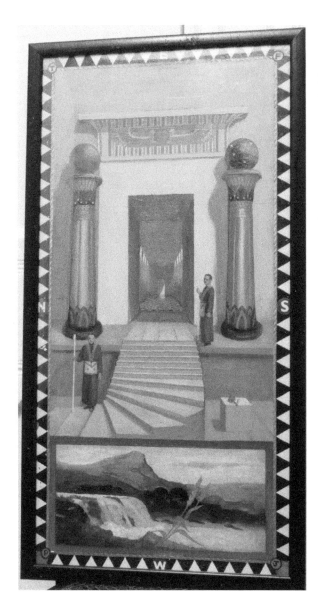

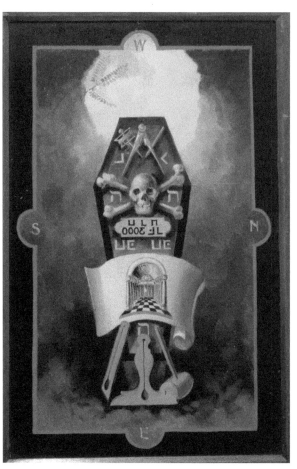

On this and the previous page: Three tracing boards of the International Order of Freemasonry Le Droit Humain

There are very few instances of tracing boards designed in and for the 20th and 21st centuries, but some outstanding examples of artistic achievement allied to intimate understanding of the symbolism are displayed by the Belgian artist and Freemason Ferenc Sebök. On the opposite page left is a combined first and second degree board designed for the Quadrum Leonardi Lodge in Budapest. It bears many of the hallmarks of the French boards we have seen: the pointed cubic stone, three windows, broad and pointed chisels and a very striking cord of union with tulip-shaped tassels. The pillars are arranged in reverse order to the English tradition. The east and west limits are designated by the letters Or(ient) and Occ(ident), in the north is the name of the Lodge and in the south the motto of the Ancient and Accepted Scottish rite *Ordo ab Chao* (order out of chaos). On the right is a third degree board designed for the Iris Lodge in Liège, featuring the tear drops of the French boards and a very strict geometrical layout. In place of the four cardinal points are the letters spelling the name of the Lodge – I, R, I and S. Here too the pillars are reversed. In the section on German carpets we saw how 20th century art had begun to take over after the Second World War – here in the 21st century, the process has gone further.

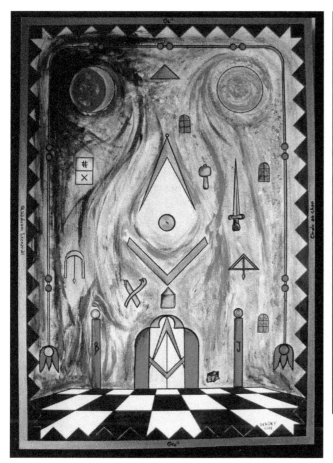

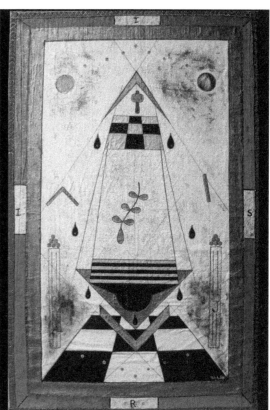

Above: Tracing board of the Quadrum Leonardi Lodge, Budapest, Hungary.

Above right: Tracing board of the Iris Lodge, Liège, Belgium

Of tracing boards designed in the 20th century, the International Order of Freemasonry Le Droit Humain gives us one outstanding example, shown on pages 92 and 93. Born in 1877, Lady Frieda Harris, the wife of Sir Percy Harris, Chief Whip in the Liberal Party in England, was a member of the Order and a friend of Aleister Crowley, for whom she designed the famous Thoth Tarot cards. It is assumed that she designed these tracing boards in the late 1930s.

In 1937 Frieda Harris began studying Projective Synthetic Geometry which was based on the teachings of Rudolf Steiner and Goethe. Parallel lines, as we know, meet in infinity, so the two grand parallel lines on the first degree board are shown as converging. Because of these same converging lines, what starts out as diamond-form pavement becomes, towards the back of the picture, conventional square-form. The blazing star or glory appears as a diamond at the top of the ladder, the symbol for charity is a chalice, but otherwise the symbols are what we are used to, with the exception of the sword. This emblem, in the ritual of the International Order of Freemasonry Le Droit Humain, is significant for more than one reason, the most important one being, at the making of a Mason, to channel the divine energy, to act as a conduit, through the Master, between the Almighty and the neophyte. In some jurisdictions the sword, aside from being a ceremonial implement, is also an emblem, not of offence, but of defence of the one by the many. In the second board the Warden is equipped with a square to test the work, with an intricate pavement in the background. The staircase itself passes the ear of corn near to a fall of water and, near its top, incorporates the five orders

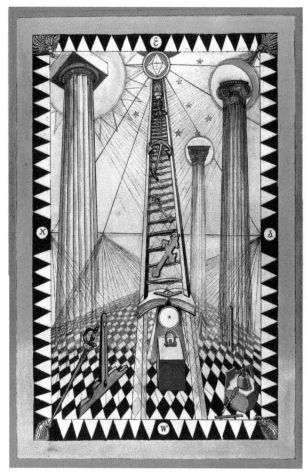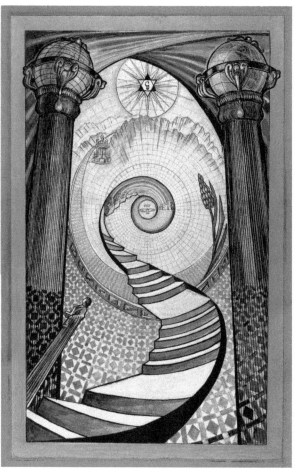

Above and opposite:
Three tracing boards
designed by Lady Frieda
Harris

of architecture curved round it, arriving at the tetragrammaton with a dove at the centre of the board. Above that and to the left is to be seen an image of a celestial palace. This may be correlated with the fifth section of the first Emulation lecture when speaking of the immovable jewels and the furniture of the Lodge:

> *... the Volume of the Sacred Law may justly be deemed the spiritual tracing board of the Great Architect of the Universe, in which are laid down such Divine laws and moral plans, that were we conversant therein, and adherent thereto, would bring us to an ethereal mansion, not made with hands, eternal in the heavens.*

The blazing star or glory and letter G appear just under a multi-coloured canopy. In the third board, not content with a single sprig, acacia branches abound, encircling the central prism-like repository of many third degree emblems. There are nine stars in the background, two at the top, and of the seven lower down, each one is accompanied by an astrological sign; reading from left to right, Mercury, Venus, Mars, Jupiter, Saturn, Uranus and Neptune. Sun and moon are shown in the top background, skirret, pencil and compasses at the top of the coffin-shaped interior, and a hexalpha in the ceiling of the Sanctum Sanctorum. The two numerals 5 are completed by one ה or Hebrew Hē. Beneath the skull and crossbones on the coffin shape are the letters MB in reverse cypher. Most strikingly, the whole complex image appears to be borne aloft on eight pairs of angels' wings.

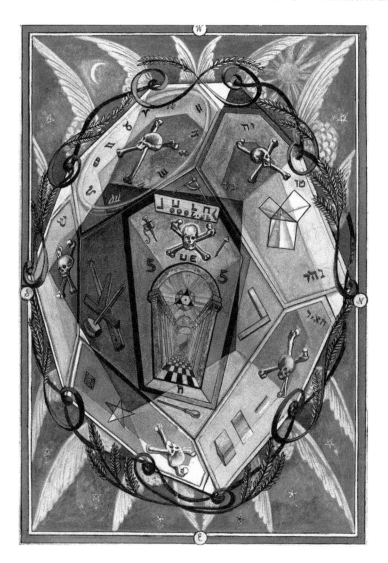

Apart from the symbols mentioned here on these last three boards, there are many more, and to the knowledge of the writer these have never been adequately researched and explored. Were there to be a fitting postscript to this work, it might perhaps be an invitation to an inquisitive and adventurous reader to undertake this virgin field of research.

FURTHER READING

The English-speaking reader should not be put off by the non-English language titles referenced here, which are all richly illustrated.

Barker Cryer, Neville, *I just Didn't Know That*,
    Lewis Masonic, 1999. ISBN 0-85318-219-1

Barker Cryer, Neville, *Did You Know This Too?*,
    Lewis Masonic, 2005. ISBN 0-85318-241-8

Curl, James Stevens, *The Art and Architecture of Freemasonry*,
    Batsford, 1991. ISBN 0-7134-5827-5

Dyer, Colin F.W., *Emulation - A Ritual To Remember*,
    A. Lewis, 1973. ISBN 9690000039165

Dyer, Colin F.W., *Symbolism in Craft Freemasonry*,
    Lewis Masonic, 1976. ISBN 0-85318-233-7

Feddersen, Klaus C.F., *Arbeitstafel in der Freimaurerei*,
    Quatuor Coronati Lodge Bayreuth, 1982. Published in Germany

Haunch, Terence O., *Tracing Boards - Their Development and Their Designers*,
    Quatuor Coronati Lodge London, 1963. ISBN 0-907655-95-5

The Lectures of the Three Degrees in Craft Masonry,
    Lewis Masonic.

MacNulty, W. Kirk, *Freemasonry – A journey Through Ritual and Symbol*,
    Thames and Hudson, 1991. ISBN 0-500-81037-0

MacNulty, W. Kirk, *The Way of the Craftsman*,
    Central Regalia, 2002. ISBN 0-954-2516-0-1

MacNulty, W. Kirk, *Freemasonry – Symbols, Secrets, Significance*,
    Thames and Hudson, 2006. ISBN 978-0-500-51302-6

Mainguy, Irène, *La Symbolique Maçonnique du Troisième Millénaire*,
    Editions Dervy, 2006. ISBN 978-2-84454-116-1

Rees, Julian, *Making Light - a Handbook for Freemasons*,
    Lewis Masonic, 2006. ISBN 0-85318-253-1

Rees, Julian, *Ornaments Furniture and Jewels*,
    Lewis Masonic, 2013. ISBN 978-0-85318-412-6

Thomas, Jacques, *Tableaux de Loges et Gravures Maçonniques*,
    Editions Dervy, 2005. ISBN 2-84454-374-X

The two 19th century American publications mentioned in Chapter 5 are kept in many Masonic museums throughout the world, and may be seen at the Library and Museum of Freemasonry in London. They are:

Jeremy Cross, *The True Masonic Chart, or Hieroglyphic Monitor*, first published in New Haven, Connecticut, in 1819.

Thomas Smith Webb, *Freemason's Monitor or Illustrations of Masonry*, first published in Cincinnati, Ohio, in 1859.

INDEX

Lightning Source UK Ltd.
Milton Keynes UK
UKHW05f0937050618
323689UK00005B/42/P